Start Your Own Small Business and Industry

Start Your Own Small Business and Industry

Written By

EIRI BOARD OF CONSULTANTS & ENGINEERS

ENGINEERS INDIA RESEARCH INSTITUTE

4449, Nai Sarak, Main Road, Delhi - 110006 (India)
Ph: 91-11-23918117, 23916431, 23840361
Fax: 91-11- 2391 6431, 2391 8117
*** E-Mail: eirisidi@bol.net.in**
***Website: www.eiriindia.org**

Sole Distributor :

INDIAN INSTITUTE OF CONSULTANTS, 4/27 ROOP NAGAR, DELHI -110007

PRINTED & PUBLISHED BY

ENGINEERS INDIA RESEARCH INSTITUTE

4449, Nai Sarak, Main Road, Delhi - 110006 (India)
Ph: 91-11-23918117, 23916431, 23840361
Fax: 91-11- 2391 6431, 2391 8117
* E-Mail: eirisidi@bol.net.in
*Website: www.eiriindia.org

DISTRIBUTED BY

SMALL INDUSTRY RESEARCH INSTITUTE (SIRI)
INDIAN INSTITUTE OF CONSULTANTS

ISBN: 81-86732-74-8

Printed in New Delhi (INDIA)

Rs. 350/-

Printed & Published by Sudhir Gupta for "Engineers India Research Institute" 4499 Nai Sarak, Main Road, New Delhi -110006

Preface

In 1997, the Abid Hussain Committee recommended the inclusion of small business and services within the fold of SSIs. Earlier industrial policy resolutions of 1948, 1956, 1977 and 1991 only refer to small scale industries, micro/tiny industries, ancillary industries (AIs), village industries, and khadi industries, not small business. We believe that small business is a wider term and should cover within its definition small scale industries too. This book focuses not only on the small scale industries, but also on small businesses in wholesale,. retail, trade as well as services.

As SSI is a production unit engaged in manufacturing goods or articles in small quantities, employing a smaller number of workers, using traditional/modern tools or machines with the lowest possible capital investment. The Factories Act, 1948, is applicable to most SSI manufacturing units.

The growth of small business enterprises (SBEs), including small scale industries in India, has been in the form of family business - or Hindu Undivided Family (HUF) firms - where owners are managers and family members take on other tasks. Such business firms exist in other communities not only in India but throughout the world. These business firms have an informal set-up with characteristics different from modern formal organizations. Blacksmiths, goldsmiths, carpenters, potters, brewers, bakers, weavers, dyers, vendors of milk products, tailors and drapers, etc., are examples of small businesses operating in urban and semi-urban areas.

The book ***Start Your Own Small Business and Industry*** *covers almost all the basic and advanced details to setup own small business industry. The book includes Introduction, Project Conception and Start-up, The Definition Phase, Planning the Project, Launching and Executing the Project,Launching and Executing the Project, Secrets of Success, Helping Hands to Your Success, Some Courses for Self-Employment,Addresses of Small Industries Service Institutes & Branch SISIs etc.*

Director

ENGINEERS INDIA RESEARCH INSTITUTE

Nai Sarak, New Delhi (INDIA)

E-Mail: eirisidi@bol.net.in

Contents-cum-Subject Index

Chapter 8

Chapter 9

1

Introduction

The term small business is not officially defined, therefore, it is not entitled to incentives, rebates or subsidies from the government, unlike the small scale industry (SSI). In 1997, the Abid Hussain Committee recommended the inclusion of small business and services within the fold of SSIs. Earlier industrial policy resolutions of 1948, 1956, 1977 and 1991 only refer to small scale industries, micro/tiny industries, ancillary industries (AIs), village industries, and khadi industries, not small business. We believe that small business is a wider term and should cover within its definition small scale industries too. This book focuses not only on the small scale industries, but also on small businesses in wholesale, retail, trade as well as services.

'Industry' is generally understood to mean a manufacturing process or activity resulting in production of goods or articles. These manufactured goods may be either for human consumption or used as inputs for intermediary goods in the form of half-finished products or ancillary products, for final processing and production.

As SSI is a production unit engaged in manufacturing goods or articles in small quantities, employing a smaller number of workers, using traditional/modern tools or machines with the lowest possible capital investment. The Factories Act, 1948, is applicable to most SSI manufacturing units.

The growth of small business enterprises (SBEs), including small scale industries in India, has been in the form of family business—or Hindu Undivided Family (HUF) firms—where owners are managers and family members take on other tasks. Such business firms exist in other communities not only in India but throughout the world. These business firms have an informal set-up with characteristics different from modern formal organizations. They have religious sanctions but are regulated by local laws. They are run by fewer people who are drawn from family members, friends and other relatives and are identified as such rather than as mere employees. The work atmosphere is permeated by unity, harmony, love and affection,. While outsiders are employed as well, they are also treated as family and the line between their professional and social lives is usually blurred. They are self-disciplined and self-controlled with a high degree of loyalty towards each other. They do not need formal rules, regulations or supervision. Blacksmiths, goldsmiths, carpenters, potters, brewers, bakers, weavers, dyers, vendors of milk products, tailors and drapers, etc., are examples of small businesses operating in urban and semi-urban areas.

It is the small business sector that has contributed to the growth of local economies with its easy access to local resources and local markets in both urban and rural areas. The SSI sector utilizes local resources and produces goods to meet the local demand and creates local self-sufficiency.

GOVERNMENT POLICY IN SSIs/SBEs

Despite the apparent cohesiveness, small business and industry in India have been defined separately. The small scale industry is identified in all official documents as a separate activity rather than a business enterprise. The Industrial (Development & Regulation) Act, 1951 (IDRA), has treated SSI as 'an undertaking', notified by the central government to provide supportive help, exemption or favourable treatment, in order to enable them to maintain their viability and strength as well as to be effective in promoting industrial economy and reducing the problem of unemployment. Other conditions that distinguish SSIs are: (*a*) smaller investments in plant, machinery or land/building; (*b*) fewer number of workers employed; (*c*) the nature, cost or quality of the product manufactured; (*d*) foreign exchange required for import of machinery; and (*e*) other relevant factor/s that may be prescribed by the Central Government. Thus the basic criterion for identifying the SSI was focused on the size of the investment in plant, machinery, land and buildings. This criterion was followed in all Industrial Policy statements made by the central government in 1956, 1973, 1977 and 1991. Through separate notifications, the central government had demarcated the limits of investment from time to time as given in Box 1.1.

There are sub-sectors of SSIs located in rural and semi-urban areas like village industries, handlooms, handicrafts and rural artisans, where the limit of investment is Rs. 50,000 or less in plant and machinery. But there is no such limit for small business enterprises yet, except that for the services sector the limit is fixed between rupees five million and 15 million.

Box 1.1: The Limit of Investment

Year	*SSI*	*AI*	*Tiny sector*
1966	750,000	1,000,000	100,000
1975	1,000,000	1,500,000	100,000
1980	2,000,000	2,500,000	200,000
1985	3,500,000	4,500,000	200,000
1991	6,000,000	7,500,000	500,000
1997	30,000,000	30,000,000	2,500,000
1999	10,000,000	10,000,000	2,500,000
2000	10,000,000	10,000,000	2,500,000

GOVERNMENT IDENTIFICATION OF SBEs/SSIs

To promote SSIs/SBEs, the central government stressed their importance in the Five Year Plans. The development strategy suggested therein is in Box 1.2.

Box 1.2 : Government Identification of Small Business Enterprise

- increased employment through labour intensive process
- lower gestation period
- easy to set up in rural and backward areas
- small/local market
- growth of local entrepreneurship
- a decentralized pattern of ownership
- foster diversification of economic activities.
- introduce new products particularly to cater to local needs
- influence the standard of living of local people
- provide equitable dispersal of industries throughout rural and backward areas

Essential conditions for growth of SSIs/SBEs

- conducive environment
- industrial climate
- developed infrastructure
- technical and financial support available on a consistent basis
- favourable government policy framework for development

The importance of SSIs in India, as a developing country, is wider. SSIs serve as milestones towards industrialization and create a new class of entrepreneurs, talented and endowed with initiative.

INDUSTRIAL POLICY STATEMENTS AND SSIs/SBEs

The central government issued Industrial Policy statements from time to time as referred to earlier, in order to give direction to the pattern of industrial development and to attain social, economic and political objectives. These directions reflect upon the role of public, private, joint and cooperative sectors in the development of large, medium and small scale industries. Table 1.1 summarizes the role assigned to SSIs/SBEs in the economy of the country.

Table1.3: Policy Statements Made Since Independence

1948: expressed concern for the problems of cottage and SSIs which, being labour intensive and employment oriented, offer many advantages for the rural economy and help decentralize the industrial sector. Thus, the importance of small enterprises, especially cottage and village industries was noted at the national economy level.

1956: emphasized the role of SSIs in the economy of the country and assigned the following tasks to them:

- large employment opportunities with low capital investment
- to meet domestic demand for consumer goods and even part of capital goods
- mobilization of capital and entrepreneurial skills in rural areas
- assistance to entrepreneurs/artisans/craftsmen in getting employment/income/reasonable standard of living
- make available foreign markets for products by taking measures to make them export oriented
- remove disparities in regional industrial development through development of SSIs providing income/employment to people in these areas
- to foster greater relationship between large scale industries and SSIs

1991: The significant contribution of SSIs designated as a dynamic and vibrant sector of the economy was noted as under :

Contd. . . .

- 55 per cent of industrial production
- 40 per cent of exports
- 88 per cent of manufacturing employment
- SSIs are leaders in the industrial sector in India
- government's New Policy Measures directed towards promoting and strengthening SSIs, Tiny Sector, and Village Enterprises
- upturn in policy stimulants and structure

Objectives:

- vitality and growth impetus to SSI sector
- to enable it to contribute in terms of
    - growth of output
    - employment
    - exports

Salient Features of New Policy:

- 24 per cent equity participation by other industrial undertakings and foreign companies
- hike in investment limits—Tiny Sector to 500,000 (at present Rs 2.5 million)
- to recognize the services sector as Tiny Sector
- support from National Equity Fund for projects up to Rs 1 million
- single window loan to cover projects up to Rs 2 million
- relaxation of certain provisions of labour laws
- factoring services through Small Industrial Development Bank of India (SIDBI)
- marketing by National Small Industries Corporation (NSIC)
- consumer goods under common brand name
- compulsory quality control for products posing risk to health
- Technology Development Cell to be set up
- Export Development Centre to be set up
- traditional village industries to be given greater thrust

(Contd). . .

- Tiny Sector priority in government purchases
- for ancillary units and Export Oriented Units (EOUs)—an investment limit of Rs. 7.5 million (now Rs 10 million)
- Incentive/Services/Subsidies package at district level

Initiatives in respect of policies related to:

1. Small Scale industries:
    - financial support
    - infrastructural facilities
    - marketing and export
    - modernization and upgradation of technology
    - promotion of entrepreneurship
    - simplification of rules and procedures
    - tapping resources
2. Tiny Sector
    - investment support
    - broadening the concept of the service sector
    - simplification of rules
3. Handloom Sector:
    - project package schemes
    - welfare package schemes
    - organization and Development scheme
    - national Handloom Development Corporation (NHDC) as nodal agency
4. Handicrafts
    - supply of raw material
    - market development support
    - expansion of training facilities to upgrade skills
5. Village Industries
    - improving quality
    - flow of capital from financial institutions (FIs)

(Contd). . .

- thrust of traditional village industries
- setting up functional industrial estates
- upgrading training programmes
- coordinating with development plans.

The government has taken action in pursuance of the industrial policy statements and has suggested the thrust areas for SSIs as summarized in Table 1.2.

Table 1.2: Thrust Areas for SSIs

- speedy modernization } both { enhances scope for
- upgradation of technology } both { expanded investment
- cheap/adequate/timely credit availability
- quality control
- draw SSI into mainstream of industrialization
- integration of Indian economy with global economy
- increasing capabilities towards competition through development of skills management

Payment Mechanism

- legislation to enforce payments in time of the dues of SSIs
- prompt payment is better than cheap credit

Factoring Services:

- already available from SBI/Canbank/SIDBI
- more banks to follow suit

Resources for SSIs:

- limited liability for non-active parties in SSIs so that they can pump in funds
- permitting 24 per cent equity participation by large corporate enterprise
- SSIs to operate as a part of large scale industries

(Contd). .

Timely and Adequate Credit:

- timely credit and financing arrangements
- single window clearance for project cost up to Rs 2 million and for working capital up to Rs 1 million

Nodal Agency:

- Small Industries Development Organization (SIDO) to act as nodal agency to support SSI in export promotion
- Export Development Centres as network of field offices to further augment export activities of SSIs
- Technology Development Cell set up in SIDO to provide technology inputs in improve productivity of SSIs
- relaxation of regulatory price mechanism for SSIs
- facilities in backward areas

Marketing Promotion: backed by government incentives through:

- cooperatives
- public sector organizations
- professional marketing agencies

Raw Material:

- allocation of indigenous raw material on need-based basis to SSI/Tiny Sector
- adequate and equitable distribution of imported raw material

Quality:

- compulsory quality control
- quality counselling and testing services
- Technology Information Centres for updated knowledge

GLOBAL VIEW OF SMALL BUSINESS

In the UK, small business enterprise has no single or precise definition but is distinguished with reference to several factors including the stages of development, the specific nature of business, the capacity to create employment, the turnover limit, eligibility to the loan guarantee scheme and tax exemption limits.

In the USA, small business administration has been established under the Small Business Administration Act, 1953, which defines small business as 'one which is independently owned and operated and not dominant in its field of operation'. In the USA, 98 per cent of these are small retail and service businesses. Small companies in the USA employ 35 per cent of the private sector workforce, possess one-fourth of their assets, produce 38 per cent of the US GNP and account for 42 per cent of business sales. These small businesses generate more than twice the number of jobs than industry does, and create more innovations than medium and large scale industries. US Government Policy towards small business is summarized in Box 1.3.

Box 1.3: US Government Policy Towards Small Business

* highly favourable or inspiring
    - reduction in progressive taxation
    - venture capital market, fully developed, provides full support to small business
    - financed by large corporations in the USA
    - largely technology-based
    - advanced computer-based technology leads to designing new products and gives an edge over global competitors

Small businesses in Europe including Germany, France, Italy and Finland, are less dynamic than those in the USA and the UK for the reasons given in Box 1.4.

Box 1.4: Small Business in Europe

- the European base of industry is smaller than the USA
- smaller market and no start-up on a large scale for innovation
- labour market in Europe in rigid due to higher wage/replacement of labour by automation and widespread unemployment
- rigid capital market is unfavourable for small business finance

Small businesses are widespread in Japan, even outnumbering those in the USA. They provide 50 per cent of Japan's industrial output and 75 per cent of its total employment, against 25 per cent and 50 per cent in the USA. Other special features are in the Box 1.5.

Box 1.5: Features of Japan's Small Enterprises

- they are smaller than those in the USA
- they are technology-based
- emphasis on R&D and innovation
- are supported by the following companies:
    - six giant multi-industry groups each based around a major bank or trading company
    - seven giant vertically integrated industry groups
    - six finance centred groups
    - three large outsiders: Sony, Honda, Pioneer
    - All the above large groups support 830,000 SSIs
- Big groups sustain themselves on the strength of SSIs
- Sub-contracting is an important type of SBE
- Two-thirds of manufacturing SSIs worth $830,000 are sub-contracting units
- Government of Japan and state-level institutions help SBEs

Small business enterprises are identified with the owner and subject to certain limitations which adhere to his/her ownership, ability and capacity. These limitations generally apply to all such enterprises irrespective of time and place or the stages of development within a developed or developing country. All over the world, small business enterprises are popular and have uniform features and qualities which are summarized as under:

1. Absence of functional management: management rests in the owner who usually lacks knowledge in production, finance and marketing management.
2. Organization structure: is small, simple and does not differentiate between the owner-manager. It is independent, flexible and traditional, compatible with a small volume of output and turnover.
3. Decision making: is faster, less formal and more personalized; lacks decisional layers and communication steps. The owner's presence does not leave much scope for delegation or sharing

of authority. He sets objectives, goals and plans to achieve them.

4. Organizational culture: owner-centred, 'top-down' culture dominates the workplace. Individuals in the workplace are related by a network of personal relationships, have self-discipline and are bound by harmony and love. Their attitudes towards each other are well-defined.

5. Control: direct supervision by owner-manager. There is no formal hierarchy in management and operations as is the case in large businesses.

6. Operations: Learning and training is job-based. There is no formal training, Most of the business knowledge is gained on the job through work experience. It serves local customers and has a limited share of the available market.

7. Investment and resources: the owner-manager invests his/her personal funds in the business.

8. Influences and growth: both internal and external influences are active in SBEs. Internal influences are confined to family members and external influences comprise commercial contacts, which in turn may or may not lead to the growth and expansion of the enterprise. Customers, suppliers, professional advisers, close and trusted business acquaintances, friends and relatives also exercise influence on the firm.

DIFFERENCE BETWEEN A SMALL AND LARGE BUSINESS

The features already highlighted are prominent and dominating. Besides these, there are more specific differences between small and large business enterprises as narrated below:

Business planning: This is required for a large business, but not necessary for a small business. A written business plan is a sheer waste of time and resources in a small business, as it depends upon informal advice. A large business has the resources to employ experts for business plans and project reports.

Business finance: Small businesses rarely use bank finance. It is the owners' money that is used as the informal risk capital in running the business. Since a bank provides a loan only when it is satisfied with the interest paying capacity of the borrower, they do not finance small businesses for the following reasons:

- they are considered risky as most of them have a high failure rate;

- SBEs do not have a track record nor a trading history, instead they have untried management which does not inspire confidence and the investment returns are not guaranteed;
- it is not cost effective for banks to provide loans to SBEs because the monitoring of loan accounts is difficult
- owner-managers of SBEs do not want to share equity capital with others.

Business growth: In terms of size and growth, small businesses grow slowly, if at all, while large businesses grow faster as procuring resources for growth is not a problem.

Business support network: SBEs do not encourage interference except support from government organizations.

Social engineering: SBEs do not address social problems but at the same time help to create new employment and ensure the equitable distribution of resources.

Transition to self-employment: SBEs offer a change of status, i.e., from employee to employer, from salary earning to profit sharing. However, in a small business, one has to spend first to earn income even though the outcome is uncertain. An owner can make his own decisions and acquire management skills through experience. A large business has the resources to hire the services of experts.

The distinctive features of a small business disappear with the pace of growth and expansion which it seeks with success, eventually changing in character to a large business.

THE IMPORTANCE OF SSIs/SBEs IN THE INDIAN ECONOMY

Small business in India is important because it offers solutions to backwardness, unemployment and the uneven income levels in the population.

India is a labour abundant and capital scarce country. SSIs/SBEs play an important role in absorbing labour in a productive activity with small capital input. They offer locational flexibility in the use of natural resources and indigenous technology. It is easier to manage industrail dispersal in rural or semi-urban areas.

SSIs/SBEs offer easy adjustment in the production process to suit the consumers' satisfaction and other requirements including personalized services with a desired degree of innovation and productiveness to suit local demand. They also provide employment near residential areas resulting in maximum efficiency and productivity.

SSIs/SBEs play a key role in industrialization due to their high labour-capital ratio, low investment, equitable distribution of national income, effective mobilization of local resources, viz., capital, skills, raw material and fostering the growth of entrepreneurs in industrially backward areas.

The economic benefits of SSIs/SBEs can be seen in Table 1.3.

Table 1.3: Economic Benefits to the Nation

---

1. Production Process:
    - cheaper technology within reach and requires a smaller amount of investment
    - labour intensive
    - project completion period is short, revenue generation is quick
    - offers training ground for local entrepreneurs
2. Local Market:
    - cheaper product
    - lower transportation cost

(Box 1.8. contd.)

- lower overheads
- meets demand for mass consumption goods

3. Large Industries:
    - Support to large industries by supplying
        - intermediary, semi-processed, ancillary and producers' goods
4. Rural Development:
    - linked to rural development and agricultural development
    - rural industry meets requirement of rural folk engaged in farming and allied activities
    - production of export oriented goods brings surplus trade balance
    - elimination of backwardness in different regions; fosters

(Contd). . .

- regional development
- self-reliance
- employment
- increased welfare/standard of living

- utilization of local resources creates increasing:
  - demand for resources
  - employment
  - income resources
- economic well-being and fosters economic justice

THE ROLE OF SSIs/SBEs IN ECONOMIC DEVELOPMENT

Economic development leads to a better standard of living, higher national income, higher per capita income, better education, secures welfare and encourages higher savings and investments. It also provides opportunities for employment. There is optimum utilization of national resources and trained human assets, which in turn generates a surplus of production; this pushes exports and enables the import of modern technology. SSIs/SBEs play a key role in achieving these objectives.

Since India is predominantly an agricultural country, SSIs/SBEs can be based on agro-products as this focus will generate employment opportunities and galvanize the rural economy. In this way cottage industries, village artisans and craftsmen will also be given a boost.

The Reserve Bank of India's (RBI) Annual Report of 1998-99 points out that: SSIs have a high potential for employment opportunities and contribute 40 per cent of the total industrial output.

On 30 June, 1998* the RBI announced an improvement in the credit delivery system and a simplification of procedures including

- an increase in the limit of composite loans from Rs 0.2 million to Rs 0.5 million;
- delegation of more powers to branch managers for granting ad hoc facilities to the extent of 20 per cent of the sanctioned limit;
- strengthening of recovery mechanisms;
- opening of more SSI bank branches;

---

* RBI: Annual Report, 1998-99, p. 33 and para 225 p. 58

- raising the excise exemption limit from Rs 3 million to Rs 5 million and setting a flat rate of 5 per cent for clearance between Rs 5 million and 10 million; and
- doubling the ceiling of bank advances for working capital to Rs 40 million.

The Union Budget 2000-01 provides the following measures to increase the employment generation capacity and export capabilities of SSIs:

1. To dispense with the collateral requirement for loans, the limit is being further increased for the tiny sector from Rs 0.1 million to Rs 0.5 million.
2. To promote credit flow to small borrowers, the composite loan limit is being increased from Rs 0.5 million to Rs 1 million under the SIDBI's composite loan schemes.
3. Public sector banks required to accelerate their programme of SSI branches to ensure that every district and SSIs within districts are served by at least one specialized SSI bank branch. Further, to improve the quality of banking services, SSI branches are now required to obtain ISO certification.
4. Credit guarantee schemes for SSI to be launched. A provision for Rs 1 billion has been made in the budget. The scheme will be through the SIDBI and will cover loans up to Rs 1 million from the banking sector.
5. The SIDBI operates the National Equity Fund Scheme under which equity support is provided for projects up to Rs 1.5 million. To further help SSI entrepreneurs, this limit will be raised from Rs 1.5 million to Rs 2.5 million.
6. The SIDBI at present administers the Technology Development Modernization Fund Scheme to assist technology development and modernization of SSI units. The scheme has certain concessional features including interest at prime lending rates for direct assistance and refinancing at 2 per cent below the prime rate for indirect finance. This scheme is being extended for another three years.
7. The Khadi and Village Industries Commission (KVIC) has played a very important role in generating large scale employment in rural areas. The government has encouraged this sector to enable its products to become more competitive. By intensifying its

marketing efforts, the KVIC has introduced a common brand name—khadi—for its products and has also set up a professionally managed marketing company for domestic as well as export marketing.

THE ENTREPRENEUR AND SMALL BUSINESS

An entrepreneur is one who translates an idea into a business enterprise. He must possess large doses of creativity, determination, initiative, self-confidence and trust to ensure success in any venture.

Joseph A. Schumpeter, economist, attributes an entrepreneur to be one who introduces (a) new methods of production in a manufacturing activity not yet tested by experience; (b) a completely new product; (c) a new source of raw material; (d) a new market; or (e) one who reforms and revolutionizes the pattern of production by exploiting existing inventions or untried technology in the production of a new commodity.

Peter Drucker, management expert, describes an entrepreneur as an 'innovator' who exploits change as an opportunity for different business or services.

Walker treats an entrepreneur as one who is endowed with more than average capacities in the task of organizing and co-ordinating the various other factors of production.

Noah Webster feels that an entrepreneur assumes the 'risk and management of business'.

Sociological conditions in India have played a key role in entrepreneurial enterprise. Social culture, social sanctions, cultural values and role expectations have been vital in setting occupational communities and demarcating the caste system that dominates the business classes. Social values determine attitude and role expectations whereas religious beliefs decide occupational pursuits. Occupation decides castes and settles communities. In India, the business communities of the Marwaris, Parsis, Gujaratis and Sindhis have fared better than others. Psychological factors in individuals originate from family culture and upbringing. These factors sometimes dictate inner thinking and influence outward behaviour. An individual's willpower helps to motivate entrepreneurial activities for which he/she undertakes risks and desires high performance.

In the stages of small business development, Churchill and Lewis have come out with 'model X' where culture and awareness is the real environment which an individual faces at home before conceiving an idea for a product or service. Culture and awareness comes from the family and religious background supplemented by education and other factors like psychological make-up, age and earlier career experience and exposure to opportunities leading to entrepreneurial efforts. These serve as antecedental influences upon the entrepreneur to generate an idea which is incubated by geographical location, required skills and knowledge, motivation and experience in setting up the business. The idea is firmed up once exposed to external factors, as discussed by Cooper, which include examples of external factors, as discussed by Cooper, which include examples of entrepreneurial action, social attitude, available seed capital, accessibility to venture capital, availability of personal and supporting services, accessibility to the customer, opportunities for counselling and economic conditions.

Based on these and other experts' views the qualities or characteristics an entrepreneur must possess have been outlined in Table 1.4

Table1.4: Characteristics of an Entrepreneur

- *Mental ability:* intelligence, organizational skills, creative thinking, ability to analyse problems or situations, find solutions, anticipate changes and take quick decisions.
- *Clear focus*: regarding the exact nature of business/goods to be produced, subsidiary activities to be undertaken.
- *Confidentiality:* maintains and preserves business secrets from competitors.
- *Human relations:* possesses administrative skills, encourages and maintains cordial relations with customers, employees, suppliers and creditors and understands the need for a stable, balanced business environment.
- *Communication*: communicates effectively with his/her peers, customers, suppliers, employees and creditors.
- *Technical knowledge:* possesses reasonable level of technical knowledge.

Other Key Characteristics

- *Motivator:* builds a team, keeps it motivated, creates environment for industrial growth and career development.
- *Self-confidence:* ability to achieve goals.
- *Long-term investment:* has the ability to sustain the business for at least five to seven years.

(Contd). . .

- *Initiative:* accepts personal responsibility for actions.
- *Moderate risk taker:* learns from failures and setbacks and accepts new challenges.

These personality traits can be observed in noted industrialists Rockefeller, Henry Ford, Jamshedji Tata, G.D. Birla, Juggimal and Kamlapat Singhania, Gujarmal Modi, Laxmanrao Kirloskar and other enormously successful entrepreneurs.

The entrepreneur's tasks are multi-dimensional and include, as owner of the business, the following:

1. ownership and control: he is the supplier of funds and is owner-manager of the business with full control vested in him;
2. exchange relationship: perceives market opportunities, gains command over scarce resources, purchases inputs, creates value in inputs, markets the product and competes for success;
3. political and administrative: deals with the bureaucracy for concessions, licences, rebates, approvals, taxes, manages human resource, and relations with customers/suppliers;
4. production and technology: oversees the factory or trade, participates in industrial engineering and production process, upgrades process and quality.

To conclude, an entrepreneur is involved in economic activity, risk taking, decision making and coordination in different areas of the work. His rewards come from his success.

Based upon his qualities and characteristic, an entrepreneur can be differentiated into various types as can be seen from Table 1.5.

Table 1.5: Types of Entrepreneurs

---

1. *Innovative:* he is aggressive, creative, introduces new techniques, and is keen to explore new products and markets.

2. *Adoptive/imitative:* found in developing countries, follows others' experiences and exploits possibilities of market and production.

3. *Fabian:* dominated by tradition, custom and religion, is cautious and sceptical of change, usually found in under-developed countries

(Contd). . .

4. *Drone:* conventional, resists change in production processes despite losses.
5. *Other:*
   - (a) individual or institutional;
   - (b) by inheritance;
   - (c) technologist: or
   - (d) forced, due to circumstance/failure in other field.

An entrepreneur with the above profile rarely fails. He can turn failure into success by changing the inner and outer environment in his favour. The reasons for failure are usually circumstances like an unfavourable business environment, slip in financial control, lack of liquidity and inventory control, inappropriate location, non-availability of resources/market and the absence of governmental support services.

How to Become an Entrepreneur

Apart from the characteristics and qualities an entrepreneur must possess, an individual may also acquire them through experience, i.e., trial and error, which can be expensive and discouraging. Training, therefore, is the preferred method through which an individual can learn to become an entrepreneur. There are various institutions at the union and state government level that provide training to build knowledge and skill. See Table 1.6.

Table 1.6: Training and Development Institutions

SIDO:	The *Small Industries Development Organization.* Entrepreneurial skills are imparted under the Entrepreneur Development Programmes (EDPs). SIDO has established the Small Industries Extension and Training Institute (SIET) at Hyderabad which runs EDPs at various centres in the country and provides training.
SISI:	The *Small Industries Services Institute* conducts programmes throughout the country at different centres.
CED:	The *Centre for Entrepreneurial Development* was established at Ahmedabad in Gujarat by the state government, which provides low cost, high quality training and comprehensive EDPs covering motivation, project counselling, management, orientation, etc.

(Contd)...

EDII: The *Entrepreneurship Development Institute of India* established in 1983 at Ahmedabad by the State Bank of India and All India Financial Institutions undertakes nodal training programmes, trains the trainers and assists state-level agencies engaged in training and EDPs.

NIESBUD & NEDB: The *National Institute of Entrepreneurship and Small Business Development* was established by the central government in 1983 as an apex body. It serves as the secretariat for the *National Science and Technology Entrepreneurship Development Board.* It conducts training programmes, assists NEDB in determining policy for EDPs. It is the apex national-level resource institute.

EGB: The *Entrepreneurial Guidance Bureau* established by the India Investment Centre conducts EDPs throughout India for potential entrepreneurs–engineering and science graduates are the main participants.

IED: The *Institute of Entrepreneurial Development* established by the Uttar Pradesh government with All India Financial Institutions at Lucknow:

(*a*) organizes: training, research and extension activities aimed at developing potential and existing entrepreneurs.

(*b*) coordinates and supports these activities in the state and adjoining under-developed areas.

(*c*) prepares trainees involved in developmental programmes, counsels and provides motivation.

(*d*) activities that help create a conducive entrepreneurial climate for the growth and development of entrepreneurs.

(*e*) helps provide information and support to institutions engaged in the promotion of entrepreneurship.

XISS: The *Xavier Institute of Social Services* has been operational since 947 at Ranchi (Bihar), working with social organizations like *Vikas Maitri,* training the rural youth in motivational and managerial traits, project preparation, market surveys and offering financial assistance and counselling.

(Contd). . .

CYSEC: *Kolkata Youth Self Employment Centre,* 1970, registered as a society by industrialists and traders, provides vocational training, assists youth in setting up their own business.

TOCs: *Technical Consultancy Organizations* have been set up by All India Financial Institutions in 17 states to render high quality advisory services/consultancy/training and comprehensive packages to small entrepreneurs. They specialize in identification of industrial projects, conduct pre-investment studies, prepare project/feasibility reports, undertake techno-economic surveys and market research.

NISIET: The *National Institute of Small Industries Extension* Training located at Hyderabad provides training to entrepreneurs.

IIE: The *Indian Institute of Entrepreneurship,* Guwahati, also runs open learning programmes in entrepreneurship all over India. It is supported by the National Bank for Agriculture and Rural Development (NABARD) and the SIDBI.

Training increases the potential ability to improve performance, minimizes the chance of failure, increases efficiency, assures better quality results, helps improve employer-employee and consumes-customer relationships and prepares the entrepreneur to accept challenges, systematize the workplace and motivate the work force towards improved performance.

Entrepreneurial training programmes are designed with special attention to achieve their objectives. Salient features found in these programmes are given in Table 1.7.

Table 1.7: Features of Entrepreneurial Training Programmes

Objectives

1. to target goals to be achieved in the organization
2. to enhance basic knowledge with regard to industry, products, methods, techniques and skills; and

- create new skills in entrepreneur/workers
- broaden their horizon through the exchange of experiences
- gain knowledge about customers and markets
- enhance productivity and efficiency

(Contd). . .

Principles of Training:

- qualified trainers who are to impart a comprehensive coverage of both theory and practical:
  - induction training
  - job training
  - reorientation training
  - promotion training

Training Methods Depend Upon:

- trainee population
- nature of learning
- trainers themselves
- time and other factors

Designing an Entrepreneurial Training Programme:

- setting up objectives
- developing course content
- selection of training methods
- training process

Elements of Content:

- subject matter
- learning points such as knowledge, habits, skills and control of emotions

Process:

- setting up training objectives
- developing course content/curriculum
- choosing a training method.

Financial and Technical Support for Training Programme:

- sponsor support
- contributory support by trainees

Mode of Training: Selection of Trainees

A. Individual instruction: an individual is selected and complicated and specialized training imparted

B. Group Instruction: a group is selected and general instructions imparted

Selection of Methods:

1. the lecture method to cover theoretical aspects through oral communication
   - practice to be followed
2. the demonstration method
   - physical performance is given
   - practical aspects are exhibited
3. the written instruction method
   - medium of training covers written course and reading references
4. the conference method: experts share their ideas and experiences and discuss new ideas/new techniques
5. meetings
   - involving groups of people
   - discuss problems faced by them
   - exchange ideas/views
   - consider proposals/ alternative

Training in Rural Areas

Rural areas have different characteristics and as the development of entrepreneurs in these areas is directed to meet rural requirements, their training needs are different.

To eradicate poverty, involve the poor in the production and income generation process of the economy, the Integrated Rural Development

Programmes (IRDP) were started throughout the country. They aim at self-employment for the rural poor, assistance in the form of subsidy by the government and term credit by financial institutions. The District Rural Development Agency (DRDA), Zila Parishad, is the implementing agency for the IRDP.

In 1982-83, the Development of Women and Children in Rural Areas (DWCRA) was launched for the economic empowerment of women in rural areas. The organization provides funds for the amelioration of women in the form of working capital and credit, training, employment, management skills, etc., to women entrepreneurs.

In order to provide basic technical and entrepreneurial skills to the rural youth, especially to those from families below the poverty line, and to enable them to be self-employed in agriculture and allied sectors, industries, services and other activities, the Training for Rural Youth for Self-Employment (TRYSEM) was introduced on August 15, 1979.

Training in rural areas is imparted through specialized institutions like the National Institute of Rural Development (NIRD). It has a well-equipped computer facility and trains senior officers, development functionaries, representatives of NGOs, etc. It also offers consultancy and publishes literature on the subject.

At the state level, the State Institute of Rural Development (SIRD) is instrumental for human resource development. SIRDs are operational in 25 states.

In addition Extension Training Centres (ETCs) impart training to village/ block-level functionaries to help raise their professional competence to serve the rural people more efficiently.

ENTREPRENEURIAL DEVELOPMENT PROGRAMMES (EDPs)

How to Select an EDP

Every EDP has five distinct stages: (*a*) selection of candidates, (*b*) content of training programmes; (*c*) availability of support systems to facilitate setting up an enterprise; (*d*) to start production applying managerial and technological skills acquired during training and to take up marketing; and (*e*) monitoring the gains of training and assessing the inter-relationship of these stages for continued guidance.

While an entrepreneur has a constructive role to play in selecting an EDP it appears that EDPs generally prefer to select people who reflect the ideal qualities and characteristics of entrepreneurs.

Therefore, while selecting an EDP, the entrepreneur should ensure that it meets with his training requirements and will supplement the skills prerequisite for the business he proposes to set up. Trainers should familiarize themselves with details like the candidate's age, education and occupation, family background and resources for investment available and his experience in trade or industry. These particulars help trainers to design training programmes for the candidates. Therefore it is important for a candidate to provide accurate information about him/herself. This includes disclosing the field of business which he/she has chosen to pursue, based upon his/her skill, experience, background and resources.

Second, the content of the training programme should define the target group for which it has been designed, i.e., entrepreneurs should be from similar backgrounds and have common objectives. It should specify the duration of the programme (usually six weeks), outline the areas of technical knowledge and skills to be covered, including cost and benefits, provide a list of industrial units for training, etc.

Third, a support system and procedure needed for establishing an enterprise should be disclosed to the participants, including the agencies which provide resources like raw material, skilled labour, finance, marketing assistance and other industrial services.

Fourth, the entrepreneur should know how to apply the knowledge, managerial and technological skills acquired during training, to real life situations when production starts and marketing takes place.

Fifth, monitoring is vital to provide continuous guidance and follow up in the post-training stage in order to assist an entrepreneur to achieve his objective. The usual practice is by maintaining separate files for each trainee containing his personal records, performance during training, traits before and after training, and supporting agencies which help the trainee in setting up his enterprise. EDP institutions also keep in touch with every entrepreneur through correspondence and periodic visits.

CLASSIFICATION OF SSIs

SSIs can be classified in different ways as under:

1. As per industry classification: food and allied industries, textiles, chemical, electrical, engineering, etc.
2. As per the reservations in Schedule III given under the IDRA.
3. As per ownership classifications like proprietary, partnership or corporate.
4. As per operational efficiency, viz.,
    - ongoing concern

4. As per operational efficiency, viz.,
   - ongoing concern
   - growth industry or sunrise industry
   - sick industry

The classification of SSIs as per points (1) and (2) above overlap. Schedule III in the IDRA contains a list of items reserved for SSIs in different industries based on industry classification. An entrepreneur may select any broad item under the list and pursue any product within a particular classification category.

To sum up, SBEs and SSIs should be treated alike except for differences which arise under the Factories Act, 1948, and other industrial legislations.

Government policy resolutions discuss the development of SSIs covering ancillary, tiny sector and rural sector industries and lay down strategies for their development with the objective to create self-employment opportunities in local areas, secure the equitable distribution of income resources and dispersal of industry on an equitable basis. For this purpose, there is stress on training of entrepreneurs through institutions established by the government and voluntary organizations. EDPs are key to the development of SBEs and SSIs and more importance is given in these programmes to instil skills in budding entrepreneurs.

2

Project Conception and Start-up

Most projects start from an initial idea, either from a potential customer or generated inside the organisation. Such ideas usually abound, far exceeding the available resources or funding for them all to be realistically turned into active projects. An initial screening process is essential if the organisation is not to over-commit resources and fail to deliver the desired results. This may involve some simple form of written proposal or just be a management decision to derive the initial business case. As a general rule it is preferable to derive the initial business case as a basis for informed decisions to be made.

SELECTING THE RIGHT PROJECT

How often do organisations pour effort and money into a project to find at the end that no-one needs the outcome? There are two fundamental approaches to the selection process:

- a model generating quantitative data;
- and a model only generating qualitative data.

Selection is ultimately the decision of the senior management through the PST who need to be given enough data by you to make that decision. Selecting the wrong project may precipitate failure. If the climate described earlier is established then a strategic fit is a prerequisite for the PST to even consider a project proposal or business case. Every organisation should develop its own way of conducting this process to ensure the total portfolio of active projects does not demand more funds or resources than can be provided to achieve success.

Figure 2.1 illustrates one approach where the PST based on an initial business case or proposal conducts the initial screening of ideas and

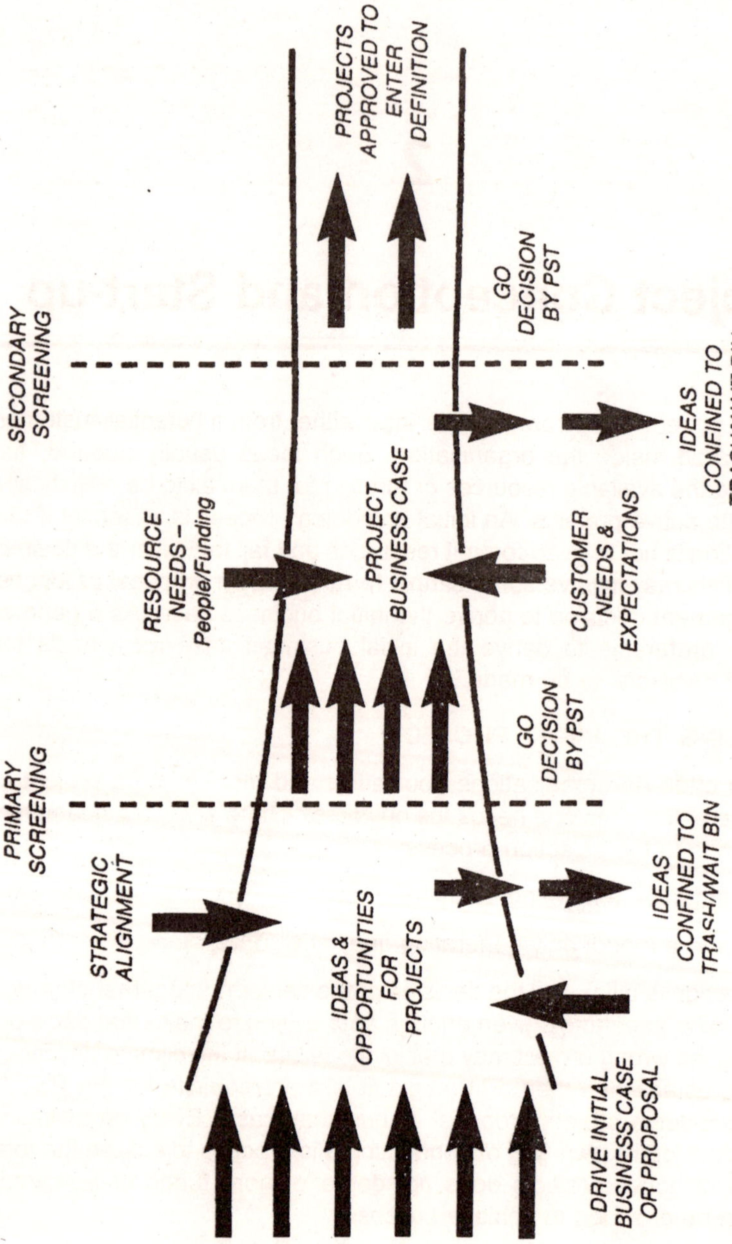

Figure 2.1: Selecting the right projects

opportunities for projects. Those approved for more detailed scrutiny are then subject to a full needs and expectations analysis by an initial core team along with a review of resource needs. This data is used to generate a full business case for the proposed project. A secondary screening by the PST reviews the full business case before opening the gate to the definition phase. At each screening some opportunities are dropped completely or confined to a 'wait bin' for later consideration.

Any project selection process will induce the PST to ask some basic questions:

- Will the proposed project maximise profits?
- Will the proposed project:
  - maintain market share?
  - consolidate market position?
  - open up new markets?
- Will the project maximise utilisation of existing resources (i.e. people)?
- Will the project maximise the utilisation of existing manufacturing capacity?
- Will the project boost company image?
- Will the project increase risk faced by the company?
- Is the project scope within the company's current skills and experience?

The model can be constructed more rigorously by weighting some factors as more important than others indicating their value in contributing to the company objectives at the time. A detailed list of factors can be developed as appropriate based on:

- technology;
- marketing;
- finance;
- manufacture;
- personnel;
- administration.

This can lead to a long list of factors which is an advantage of this approach, and if these factors are then weighted a complex model can

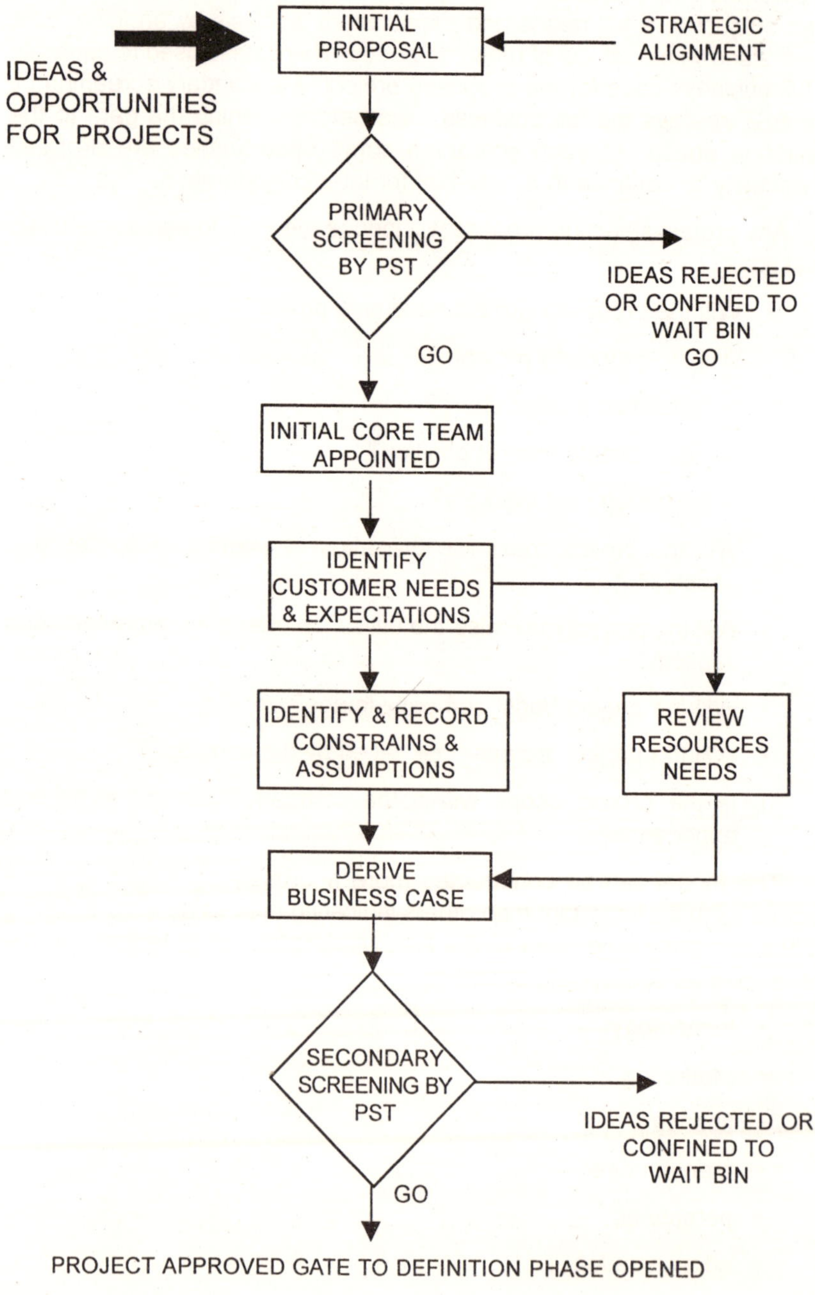

Fig. 2.2: The Start-up Process

be derived that provides a score at the end. Such a model can readily be automated as a Web-based tool making it easy to apply sensitivity analysis to any of the factors.

Quantitative Models

Most quantitative models will focus on financial data to support the case. The data generated varies widely but may include information on:

- return on investment;
- return on net assets;
- breakeven and payback period;
- cost of risks;
- net present value and/or internal rate of return;
- cost/benefit analysis;
- sensitivity analysis;
- market data.

Each of the financial techniques has its merits and disadvantages so it is common to use more than one of the above. The more data generated, the more effort required later to re-validate and measure actual performance when all the focus is on the project work.

As more information becomes available through the project, complete and enhance the data in the business case. Do pay attention to your configuration management and record all revisions or additions made. It is important that the PST always refers to the latest revision when revisiting their decisions.

THE STARTUP PROCESS

You are enthusiastic and keen to dive in and get going and show some activity. It is prudent to review just what information you can now assemble to ensure the project does not set off in the wrong direction. At this stage you should have clarified:

- who your sponsor is;
- who the customer and possible secondary customers are;
- who will use the results;
- the initial project core team – or likely candidates;
- other people who can influence the project – the stakeholders.

Your efforts and the work of the team will now be focused on gathering information from this group of individuals to kick-off the project.

Customer Needs and Expectations

Defining the needs of the customer starts off a process that will ultimately allow you to produce deliverables specifically designed to meet the customer's expectations. Once you have established a clear understanding of the needs you can develop the requirements that drive the planning process.

Working with your customers can be frustrating. At times you will need to exercise all your communication skills to achieve a good, open relationship enabling the project to move ahead to achieve the agreed objectives. Deriving the needs statement is a product of a partnership between you and your customer. This places an obligation on your customer to enter into the partnership with a serious intent to contribute openly and not sit on hidden agendas.

Exploring the needs of the customer will ultimately allow you to produce the list of deliverables specifically designed to meet the customer's expectations. Once you have established a clear understanding of the needs and validated these with the customer you can develop the requirements that drive the planning process.

Regard this as the preparation of the foundations of your project. Failure to give this activity appropriate time and effort will have continual impact on the project throughout its life.

You must make a particular effort to:

- understand the customer–explore priority and relative importance to other activities;
- understand the customer's environment in which they must operate;
- use political skills–not all customers are equal and some needs cannot be addressed;
- demonstrate your technical competence and awareness of their technical needs;
- convert ill-defined needs into practical solutions;
- keep an open mind and a creative approach;
- analyse the mixed signals you receive through personal influences on needs;
- attempt to expose the hidden expectations.

Your purpose at this stage is to turn the information you receive into a clear *statement of need* that you can reflect back to the customer for validation and acceptance with no ambiguity. Then both you and the customer are ready to collaborate fully to drive the project to a successful conclusion.

Avoid these potential traps:

1. Do not offer gold when silver is adequate–avoid striving for technical perfection beyond current capability or known state of the art. Simplicity is often more effective. Confirm that the customer understands the risks of going for leading edge solutions.
2. Effect of bias filters–it is easy for you to ignore needs for which you cannot think of an easy solution because it is outside your experience or knowledge.

CHECKLIST

Build a checklist of questions to ask your customer(s) when you start to build the business case for the project:

- What changes are identified?
  - process changes?
  - behaviour changes?
- Are these just a 'quick fix' or a quantum leap?
- What does the customer believe is needed?
- Do all customers agree?
- Have the fundamental needs been separated from wishes?
- Are predetermined solutions being proposed already?
- Has the end users perception of needs been identified?
- Have the needs been listed as primary, secondary and hopes?
- Has this list been prioritised and agreed with the customer?
- Can you turn the information into clear 'statements of need'?
- Can you use the needs analysis to derive a 'statement of requirements'?
- Will the customer agree with your statement of requirements?

(Contd)...

(Check List contd.)

Add any additional questions you can to this list:

____

____

____

____

____

____

____

You will need much of this data when you get to the next key step of defining the project.

The Customer 'Contract'

As project manager you have an obligation to turn your relationship with the customer into a form of contract. Often this is not a formal document signed by all parties but is an informal understanding. You may consider it appropriate to document some form of agreement on the obligations of yourself and the customer, focused on achieving the agreed outcomes. This will lead you to define the roles and responsibilities of both parties to the contract, to carry out the project work.

Many projects acquire a reputation for poor management when the reality is poor customer performance in fulfilling their obligations. Success is only possible if everyone involved fulfils their responsibilities and the customer cannot claim it as their right to act in complete independence. You must meet the customer requirements with constant attention to the triple constraints of project work-scope, cost and schedule. This is only possible if the customer acts promptly when necessary in resolving issues and giving approvals. Delays and cost over-runs occur too easily if customer response is slow. It suggests the customer is not so interested in getting the results of the project on time.

The project does not end with hand-over. You must check that the critical period after this phase is defined clearly for maintenance and service activities to check that the customer agrees who is responsible. Ensure these are design activities included in your project plan.

IDENTIFYING THE PROJECT CONSTRAINTS

The constraints limit all project activities. In today's business environment it is rare for you to have unlimited resources, funding and time to complete the work. The project may yield significantly reduced benefits if you provide the results at a time when the requirements or the market needs have changed dramatically.

Business and market needs are continually changing. Even with an internal project, late completion may lead others to conclude the whole effort was a waste of time, because of new requirements. Project 'drift' sets in and you face what seems like a never-ending project, trapped into acquiring a legacy of the 'project manager with the endless project'.

Constraints usually fall into categories:

- financial – project cost, capital costs, materials, revenue and resource costs;
- time – to deliver the results, the critical date when the results are needed;
- quality – the scope, specifications and standards to be achieved.

You need to explore each with your customer to gather the information you need to guarantee success. You will find that the customer will often be unable to answer your questions, arguing that it is part of the project work for you to uncover the answers.

Assumptions

It is inevitable at the start up of any project that you will make many assumptions about various aspects of the project. These are usually associated with the areas of greatest unknowns or complexity. Assumptions are potential sources of future roadblocks, so ensure that you do record them now and in the future as more get made.

At some point in your project you must validate every assumption or they will become issues to be resolved. The assumptions have no value later as excuses for failing to do something because either you or someone else forgot that it had been assumed and was never recorded. In addition the PST needs to know what assumptions have been made to help them with decision processing. It is easy in a climate that encourages you to get going with the project to ignore them and just take the view 'We'll deal with that later'.

The Kick-off Meeting

Hold a kick-off meeting. This meeting is the first time you collect together the team with other key people who have an interest in the project. It is an opportunity for you to demonstrate your ability to lead the project team. Good preparation is important to achieve the meeting purpose. Avoid diving into too much detail at this state–that will come later. Focusing on one area in detail will divert the meeting and not fulfil the meeting purpose.

The project sponsor should chair and open the meeting to explain the strategic context of the proposed project. Explain why the project is important now and how it is ranked in contrast to other active projects. Your purpose is to gain as much information as possible at this stage by asking questions.

Issue an agenda for the meeting before the meeting to give attendees time to prepare. The customer and end user may bring two or three people to the meeting, but it is better to keep the group size down to a minimum where possible.

Some typical questions to ask at the kick-off meeting include:

Background

- Why is the project necessary?
- What is the overall problem or opportunity being addressed?
- Has the current situation been explored and understood?
- Has a statement of requirements been derived from the needs list?
- Is this an old problem?
- How long has it existed?
- Who wants to change things?
- Have previous attempts (projects) been made to address this problem?
- What information exists about pat attempts to fix things?
- What assumptions have been made?

Context

- Is the project in line with current organisational strategy?
- Does the project form part of a program of projects?
- Will the project form part of a chain of linked projects or a program?
- What is the timescale of the project?
- Is there a business critical date to get the results?
- Will the results be of value to another customer or part of the organisation?

Approach

- Have all the needs been identified and analysed?
- Has a statement of requirements been agreed?
- Are there predetermined solutions?
- What are these solutions?
- Is there a best option and a least worst option?
- Is there enough time to explore more than one option?
- Are there known checkpoints for project review other than the phase gates?
- What specialised skills are expected to be required for the project work?

Objectives

- Are the project primary deliverables known?
- What does the customer need, want and wish to get from the project?
- Can these deliverables be clearly defined and specified?
- Does the end user agree with these deliverables?
- What does the end user need, want and wish to get from the project?
- What are the perceived project benefits?
- Have these benefits been quantified?
- Has a project budget been fixed?
- Is capital investment necessary?
- Has a capital expenditure request been initiated?
- Is time used for project work to be measured and costed?
- How were the costs derived?
- Has a cost/benefit analysis been carried out?
- Has a financial appraisal been carried out to establish payback?

Constraints

- Have the project constraints been identified?
- Is there a time constraint for all or part of the deliverables list?

- Is there a time constraint for all or part of the deliverables list?
- Are there any financial constraints, for example, manufacture cost, project cost?
- Is there a financial payback constraint?
- Are there any known technical constraints, for example new or untried technology?
- Are there known resource constraints?
- Is the project team to be located together on one site?
- Is part of the work to be carried out at another site?
- Is part of the work to be carried out by sub-contractors or suppliers?
- Is there a preferred list of approved sub-contractors and suppliers?
- What existing specifications and standards are to be applied to the project?
- Are there any legal constraints that might affect the project work?
- Are there any security implications?
- Are there any operational constraints, for example, access to production areas/test equipment etc.?
- Are there any Health and Safety constraints?

The data collected from these and other questions you can add will help you prepare a comprehensive business case. Your objective is to create a document that demonstrates:

- a clear understanding of the customer needs;
- what you can achieve to satisfy those needs;
- an assessment of the potential risks;
- what benefits the project could provide the organisation;
- an indication of the timescales involved;
- an assessment of the costs and return on investment involved.

The business case is not a one-off exercise as you will be required to review, validate and update, if appropriate, the contents at each phase gate until the project is complete.

RECORDING ESSENTIAL INFORMATION

You are not alone–no one likes having to record information in a regular and organised manner. Project work produces a large amount of data and it is important that you record essential material. One of the greatest timewasters in project work is repeating the recording of information in different formats, creating problems in its interpretation later.

Start off your project by avoiding the 'I'll do it my way' syndrome. Insist that the team keep all essential project records on a standard set of templates derived specifically for the purpose.

All these templates can be designed on a computer and networked for ease of completion from blank masters and given a standard distribution list. It is a good idea to give one of your team responsibility for configuration management to ensure there is always good version control of all documents.

3

The Definition Phase

THE PROJECT BRIEF AND SPECIFICATION

The data you collect from the kick-off meeting should enable you to draw up a preliminary statement of the project objectives and the associated specifications. This step is often the most difficult because you must now formulate in realistic terms just what the project is about and what it has to achieve. This is the foundation of project definition.

The *project brief* is a document that summarises all the relevant facts about the project and is, therefore, a source of definitive information. The contents include:

- the project origins–a need or opportunity statement;
- the project rationale–why is it necessary now?
- the benefits of the project–to the customer and your organisation;
- the project budget if known at this stage;
- the current timescale and expected deadlines–subject always to detailed planning later.

This document is ideally just one piece of paper, but for larger projects it often takes the form of a report with many different sections. The former is best as it forces you and the team to focus on real facts and not hopes or wishes. Unfortunately during the start-up of most projects there is too much expression of hopes and the 'wish list'. You have to resolve this conflict to sort out what you can achieve in practice with current technology, experience and knowledge that is compatible with the statement of requirements.

The project specification is a term applied to many different types of documents and can include almost anything. Here the term specification describes any document that is an obligatory statement of procedures or processes that apply to the project. It is a statement of policy for the project.

DEFINING THE PROJECT

You may ask at this point 'What is the difference between startup and definition?'. The first is a data gathering activity. Definition is the process of turning the data into something that is no longer just a wish or a hope. Failure to give adequate time to this activity and derive all the relevant data for this foundation will lead to a poorly defined project with a considerably reduced chance of achieving a successful outcome.

What is Necessary to Define a Project?

This definition phase is where many projects go wrong–often because there is no clear definition or it has remained confused with so many different stakeholder inputs. Remember successful definition must involve all the team at every step, to build their acceptance and commitment to the work of the project.

Exercise

Having conducted a kick-off meeting what do you need to write down now to define your project? List what you consider is essential information:

____

____

____

____

____

____

____

____

Everyone has their own ideas about what constitutes a definition but your purpose here is to ensure that everyone understands:

- what you intend to provide from the project;
- what you do not intend to provide;
- when the outcomes are to be provided;
- what constraints you have identified;

- what risks are involved.

Is this what you have written down? Your objective now is to:

- use the data gathered about customer needs and expectations;
- turn these needs into requirements–what you believe satisfy the needs;
- derive a project definition to specify these requirements;
- ask your customer to approve this definition.

Before you call the team together to define the project open the business-case document and review the initial data recorded. Some details may now have changed and you will need to draw any variances to the attention of the PST when you have completed the definition. The definition process is given in Figure 3.1.

A Project Organisation Chart

Draw up a list to show who is involved in the project, recording:

- name and job title/position;
- location;
- contact telephone/fax number and e-mail address;
- date assigned to the project;
- name of their line manager and contact data;
- distribution list.

Date the document and issue to everyone who needs to know–this is an essential communication document for resource planning. It ensures there is clarity about who is committed to the project. Ensure the line managers of everyone in the team receive this information–they are stakeholders and need to confirm their commitment by agreeing to these new assignments.

A Stakeholder List

Identify all those with an interest in the project–the stakeholders. The identification and management of stakeholders is a key activity for your success. It is suggested you read though Chapter 4 now before proceeding any further with definition. Create a stakeholder list, recording:

- name of stakeholder and job title/position;
- location and contact data (telephone/fax/e-mail);

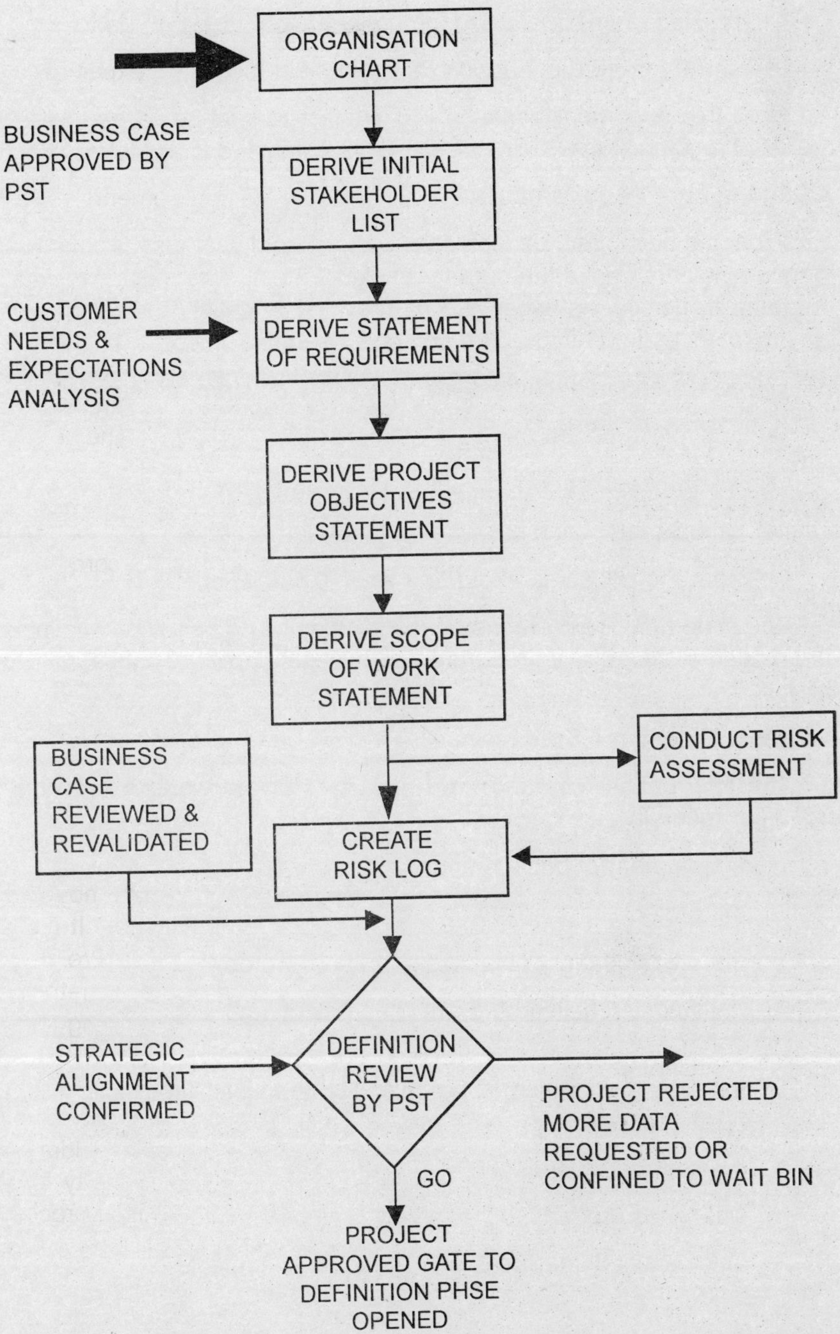

Figure 3.1: The Definition Process

- whether internal/external to your organisation;
- ranking of importance to the project (high, medium, low);
- current degree of support for the project (positive, negative?).

Date this document because it is subject to change as you review the list at regular intervals. Ensure the list is distributed to all stakeholders.

A Statement of Requirements

From the needs and expectations derived from your discussions with the stakeholders derive the data for this document. This must involve all the team to decide just what can be provided to satisfy the needs and may take several meetings. The document should record:

- needs and expectations identified and to whom attributed;
- how these needs can be met in practice;
- which needs cannot be satisfied yet and why;
- what assumptions have been made at this state;
- what the project is about and what is not included.

The statement must always be qualified as being based on available information at the date of preparation as new data may become available later.

A Project Objectives Statement

The information recorded here must be derived working with your customer recording:

- a statement of background;
- the project purpose – why are we doing this now?
- the overall project objective – in 25-30 words;
- the primary deliverables of the project with expected delivery dates;
- the primary benefits to be gained – quantified financially in the business case;
- the cost of the project;
- what skills are required – particularly those not currently available;
- any identified interfaces with other active projects.

Ensure all deliverables and benefits satisfy the SMART test:

Specific—clearly defined with completion criteria;

Measurable - understood metrics are available to identify delivery;

Achievable - within the current environment and skills available;

Realistic - not trying to get the impossible with many unknowns;

Timebound - is limited by a delivery date based on real need.

It is also valid to identify any important aspects of your proposed strategy for the project, for example:

- examining several options;
- using sub-contractors for part of the work (where skills are missing);
- using consultants for support and advice;
- re-using known methods, processes or technology.

If preferred this data can be included in the *scope of work statement.*

A Scope of Work Statement

This is a convenient place to record other useful data and cross-references to past reports and relevant projects. The document also includes:

- the project boundary limits identified–what you are not going to do;
- the standards and specifications that are applicable;
- internal product specifications;
- external product specifications;
- mandatory standards imposed by legislation;
- process specifications;
- customer specifications;
- standard operating procedures;
- purchasing procedures;
- quality standards;
- testing specifications and procedures;
- sub-contract terms and conditions imposed on third parties;

- any exceptions to these standards;
- where the standards and specifications are kept for reference;
- how success is to be measured;
- assumptions made in the project.

The scope of work statement is a useful place to locate any other relevant information that supports and clarifies your definition.

A Risk Assessment

There are risks to all projects and *risk management* is the process of identifying and containing them to ensure your project is a success. What is a risk?

> ***Definition***
>
> In project work any event that could prevent the project realising the expectations of your stakeholders is a risk. A risk that happens becomes an *issue* that must receive prompt attention to maintain the project schedule on time.

A risk assessment at this stage of a project may kill the project – through identifying such a high level of risk compared to other potential projects that it is not good business sense to continue. Three fundamental categories of risks are always present:

- *business risks* – the viability and context of the project;
- *project risks* -- associated with the technical aspects of the work to achieve the required outcomes;
- *process risks* – associated with the project process, procedures, tools and techniques employed to control the project.

As project manager, it is your obligation, working with your team to:

- identify and evaluate potential risks;
- obtain agreement to action plans to contain the risks;
- take the actions and monitor the results;
- promptly resolve any issues arising from risks that happen.

Keep your Head – Don't go Wild!

Project managers often complain that risk management is negative and an infinite process–you do not have to try too hard to come up with an enormous list of potential risks. There is no real value in listing risks you know just cannot be controlled by you or your team. Do not list 'acts of God' such as war, flood, earthquakes etc. Similarly many perceived risks in the economy and market place will have an eventual consequence for you but you cannot control these directly. Clearly some measure of judgement must be exercised when listing such risks to focus on those that may have a rapid and direct impact on your project. Then you can decide any mitigation action you could recommend if they seem likely to occur.

When is it Necessary?

Risk management is a *continuous process* throughout the life cycle of the project and you must keep all the team focused on the risks:

- start now at the definition phase;
- it is essential to establishing the *definition;*
- compile a complete list as a *project risk log.*

Review the project risk log at regular intervals, normally monthly at project progress meetings. Focus this review on:

- any change in the potential impact or probability of identified risks;
- any risks changed from previously lower ranking are then subjected to closer examination;
- deriving contingency plans for either avoidance and/or damage limitation;
- adding any new risks identified to the list and assessing these for impact and probability.

A risk entered on the list is *never* removed, even if the time zone when it could occur has passed. Your list of risks is a source of valuable learning data for future projects and is a useful data source for deriving checklists.

GETTING YOUR PROJECT DEFINITION APPROVED

The final step in the definition process is to present your documented definition to the project sponsor and your customer for approval to go on to the planning phase. At the same time you should confirm the strategic alignment and review the business case to check there are no significant changes required that impact the viability of the project.

Start by checking you have done everything you can at this stage to clearly define the project by asking some questions:

- Is the project organisation clearly established?
- Is the customer identified?
- Are roles and responsibilities at all levels understood and accepted?
- Are project accountability and authority statements issued?
- Is the corporate and strategic context and priority of the project understood?
- Has a project organisation chart been prepared and issued?
- Has a statement of requirements been derived?
- Has the project stakeholder list been prepared and issued?
- Has a project need/purpose/opportunity statement been agreed?
- Has all the relevant background information been collected?
- Is there an agreed overall project objective statement agreed?
- Is there a business critical date for the completion of the project?
- Are the project deliverables clearly identified?
- Have the project benefits been established?
- Has the project approach and strategy been agreed?
- Is the project related to other projects?
- Have the project risks been identified and quantified so far?
- Has a project risk log been prepared?
- Has a scope of work statement been prepared?
- Have all assumptions made so far been documented clearly?
- Are existing communication procedures acceptable for the project?
- Has the alignment with current strategy been confirmed?
- Has the business case been reviewed and updated where necessary?

Now you can seek the approval of your sponsor and customer. If possible use the opportunity to hold a team and stakeholder meeting for this definition review. The sponsor will present the outcome to the PST for them to approve the definition and open the entry gate to the planning phase. This approval opens the way for planning effort to proceed.

4

Planning the Project

Successful planning does not just happen and many projects induce potential failure because of a perceived need to 'get on with doing the work'. Planning is a process of creating order out of apparent chaos, made complex by the environment in which you are operating. Give time to the planning process to avoid significant re-work later. Planning is about asking questions:

- What actions need to be done?
- When are these actions to be done?
- Who is going to do them?
- What equipment and tools are required?
- What is not going to be done?

The purpose is to convert the contents of the project definition documents into a time-based plan of action that everyone understands. This enables you to achieve the results on time, to the budgeted cost and to the desired level of quality. Project planning is carried out to:

- identify everything that needs to be done;
- reduce risks and uncertainty to a minimum;
- establish standards of performance;
- provide a structured basis for executing the work;
- establish procedures for effective control of the work;
- obtain the required outcomes in the minimum time.

Planning is a dynamic and continuous process to enable you to remain proactive throughout the project.

A COMMON MISCONCEPTION

Planning is frequently regarded as just deriving a bar chart showing key activities against time–a form of schedule. This is just one part of the plan. Success with your project depends on a comprehensive plan that contains many other parts:

- a project schedule;
- a work breakdown with definitions of the work to be done;
- a resource analysis;
- a project budget;
- a communications plan;
- a quality/performance plan;
- risk management plans;
- an issue management process;
- a schedule of milestones.

At some time during the project all these are required and each should preferably be derived initially in the planning phase.

WHO NEEDS TO THE INVOLVED?

You and your project core team together. Planning is essentially a participative activity that contributes to team building and creates team 'buy-in' to the plans derived–this commitment is essential to success. Before you start your first planning session, review the skills and experience of the team members. If appropriate, invite experts from other departments to join you, stressing this is not committing them to project work later and you value their input to your efforts. Persuade your project sponsor to attend and open the planning session, explaining the project strategic context, relevance and priority. Consider inviting some of your key stakeholders if they can add value.

WHERE DOES PLANNING START?

This is always a subject of debate and argument. If the customer has an expected completion date, should you fix the completion date and work backwards? Before going any further, some terms we use need to be defined:

> ***Definitions***
>
> **A task** - a (relatively) small piece of work carried out by one person.
>
> **An activity** - a parcel of work of the project comprising several tasks, each of which may be carried out by different people.
>
> **Key stage** - a collection of activities with measurable output, often confined to a functional area.
>
> **Concurrent activities** - activities (or tasks) that are designed to be carried out in parallel, ie at the same time.
>
> **Series activities** - activities (or tasks) that are designed to be carried out one after another, each strictly dependent on completion of the earlier activity.
>
> **Duration** - the real time in working hours, days or weeks that a task or activity will take to complete.

Successful planning is a process of identifying sufficient detail to maximise concurrency and derive the shortest time to complete the project. You start by identifying the key stages of your project. These outputs may be deliverables or interim deliverables.

IDENTIFYING THE KEY STAGES

Two approaches are frequently employed, depending on the size and complexity of the work:

- ***Top down*** - listing all the interim and final deliverables of the project as outcomes from a collection of activities that forms a key stage.
- ***Bottom up*** - identifying as many activities as possible and the grouping related activities together to form the key stage.

Both methods are acceptable and successfully employed by project teams. The choice is personal preference. Top down is preferred for larger complex projects initially, followed by using the bottom-up method to identify all the tasks in each key stage.

Top-down Method

Write out the list of final deliverables as defined during project definition. Identify all the interim deliverables that must be produced to reach the point of completion of that deliverable. Remember that a deliverable or interim deliverable must be measurable - apply the SMART

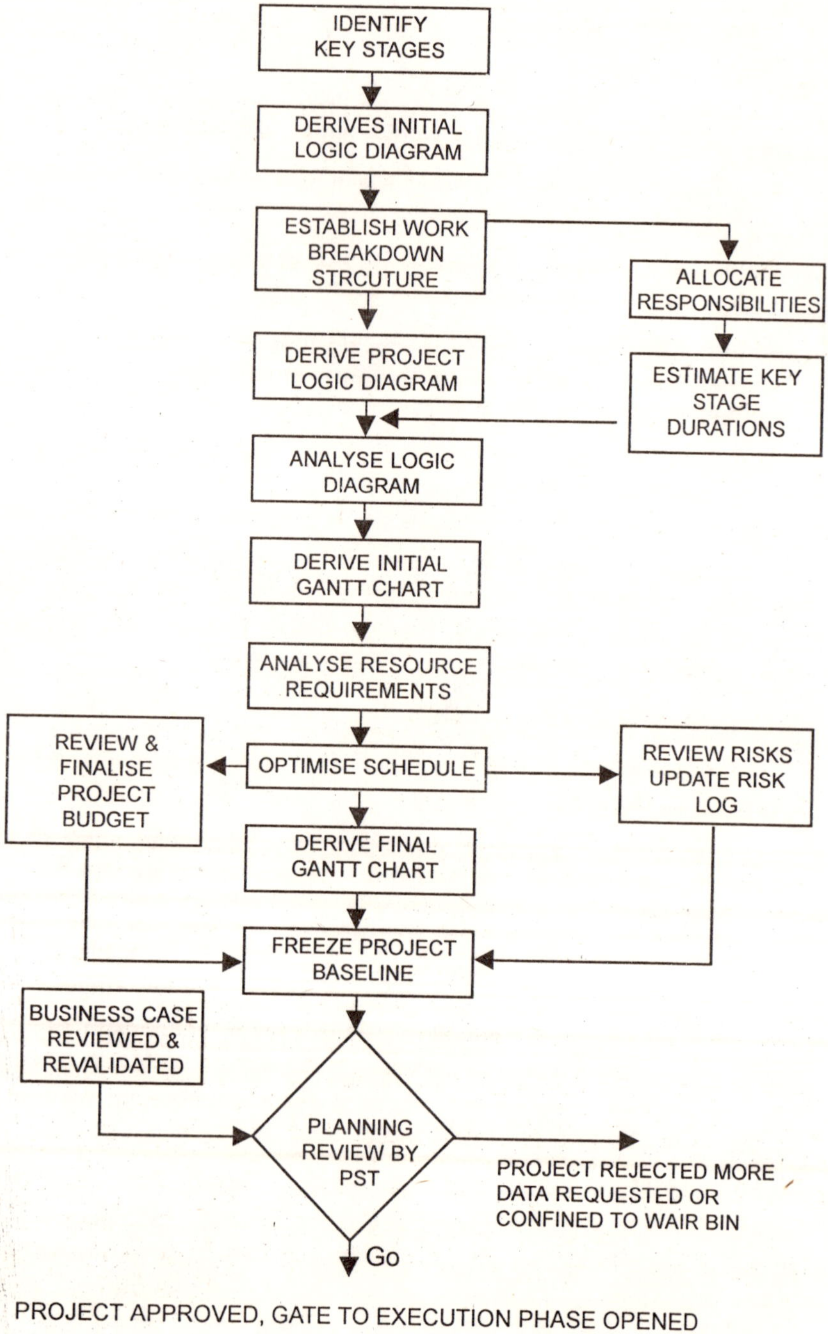

Fig. 4.1: The Planning Process

test again. This list will become your initial list of key stages, each having a defined output for another part of the project. Later we will examine how these are related to each other, as they are rarely just a set of series activities.

Bottom-up Method

Use the collective experience and knowledge of your project team and others invited to the planning session, to identify the work as a list of activities (or tasks) to be done. This is carried out in a brainstorming session. Write everything down on a flip chart and when carrying out these sessions remember to follow the basic rules of:

- quantity before quality–even if the same tasks appear more than once;
- suspend all judgement–disallow any critical comments.

Reduce your task list to a reasonable number of activities, preferably in the range of 30-100 depending on the size of the project. These are the *key stages* of your project from which everything else is developed. When clustering activities, look for measurable outputs again. Do not get concerned that there are forgotten activities. The advantage of using the key stage planning approach is that forgotten activities lose significance for the moment as they are hidden away. You can return to the detail later. This approach generally helps you identify most of the possible concurrency now and gives you an activity list that is relatively easy to manipulate.

Using the Key Stages

Once the key stages are known and agreed you organise them into a logical sequence to maximise concurrency. There are some potential traps here for you: avoid considering real time or dates yet; and avoid assigning people or functions to the key stages. Both will lead you to create errors in the project logic. Your purpose is to generate logical dependency–which key stage is dependent on which.

The next step is to derive the *project logic diagram.* This is done using a technique known as taskboarding. Write each key stage on a separate small card or self-adhesive notelet sheet. Use these as parts of the project 'jigsaw' to build the picture. Arrange them in the right logical order either on a table, using a whiteboard or simply use the office wall. This is achieved by taking each key stage in turn and asking:

What must be completed before I can start this work?

Start with the first key stages that start from a card labelled START. Continue working from left to right until all the notelet sheets have been used. Connect all the notelets with arrows to show the logical flow of the project from start to finish. Some may require inputs from more than one key stage and others may create an output that is used as input for more than one key stage.

The advantage of this technique is that everyone can be involved. The graphic impact of the diagram developing makes each member of the team question and debate the validity of the logic as it grows. Developing the logic on the wall allows everyone to see it at the same time.

The step-by-step process to derive the logic is:

- time flows from LEFT to RIGHT;
- there is no TIMESCALE on the diagram;
- place a START notelet at the extreme left of the sheet;
- place a FINISH notelet at the extreme right of the sheet;
- prepare a separate notelet for each key state;
- start each key stage description with a verb (present tense);
- do not attempt to add durations for the key stage yet;
- use different colour notelets if appropriate for different functional activities;
- locate the notelets on the sheet in order of dependency–debate each one;
- when all the notelets are used, validate the dependencies–try working back;
- show the dependency links as FINISH to START relationships initially;
- do not take people doing the work into account–it can produce errors;
- draw in the dependency links with straight arrows *in pencil;*
- avoid arrows crossing as it leads to confusion;
- label each key stage with an alphanumeric code: AB, AC, AD etc;
- do not use I or O (to avoid confusion with one or zero);
- when satisfied it is correct RECORD THE DEPENDENCIES;

if appropriate, tape the notelets down to the sheet then roll it up for filing.

The golden rule of planning applies–always use a pencil and have an eraser handy!

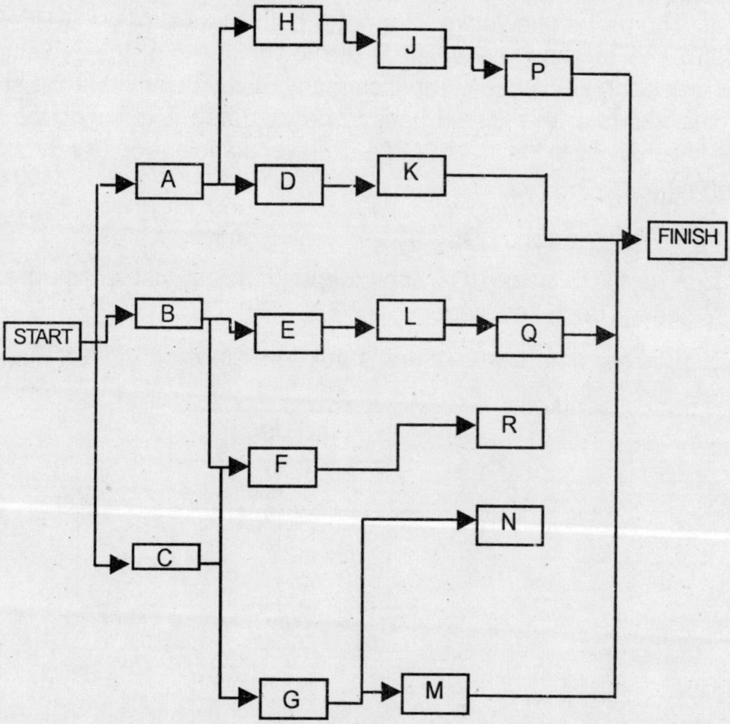

Figure 4.2: The project logic diagram

Note that the logic diagram is continuous, in other words, every key stage has at least one arrow entering (an input dependency) and at least one arrow leaving (an output dependency). To assure integrity of the logic this rule must be maintained otherwise the plan will contain errors. Of course it is not unusual to find more than one arrow depicting dependency entering and leaving some key stages.

Note also that a fundamental property of the logic is that a new activity cannot logically start until all immediately previous activities finish. If you find on reviewing the logic that a following key stage can start earlier than the end of the previous key stage, the latter must be split to show that earlier dependence. The key to successful scheduling using this logic diagram is to ensure you have well defined dependencies.

THE PROJECT WORK BREAKDOWN STRUCTURE

The *work breakdown structure* (WBS), is a convenient means of graphically presenting the work of the project in a readily understandable format. The project key stages form the highest level of the WBS which is then used to show the detail at the lower levels of the project. You know that each key stage comprises many tasks identified at the start of planning and later this list will have to be validated. Expanding the WBS to the lower levels is the process of multi-layer planning you use throughout the project.

Note that:

1. The WBS does NOT show dependencies, just a task grouping under each key stage.
2. It is not time based–there is not time scale on the drawing.

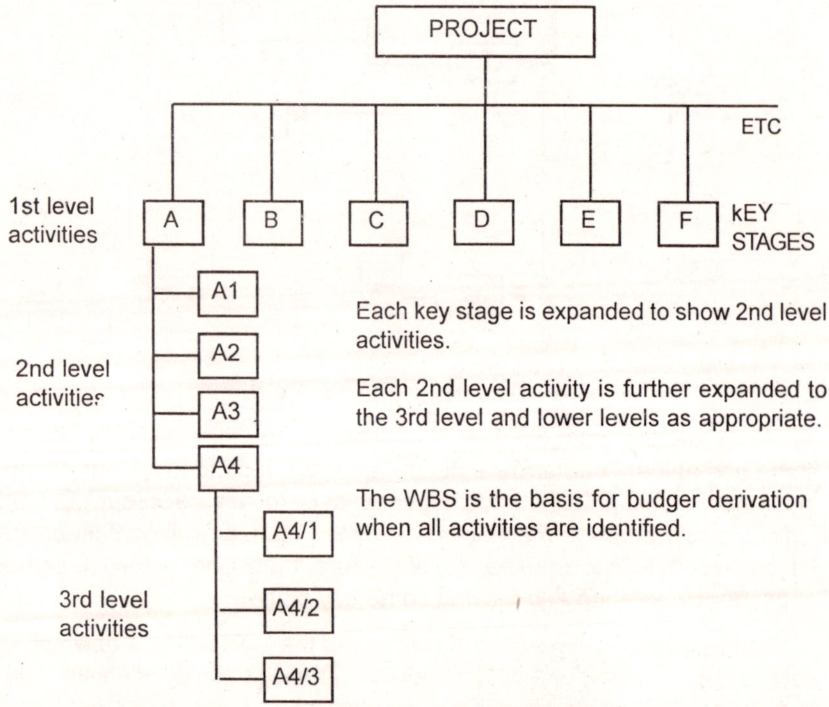

Figure 4.3: The Work Breakdown Structure.

The WBS is normally generated from project scheduling software once you have input the logic data.

ALLOCATING RESPONSIBILITY

Allocation of responsibility is essential to make sure the work is done on time and your objective is to distribute fairly and evenly the work in the team. Each of the key stages of the project needs to be owned by one of your team members. Persuade each members of the team to accept the role of *key stage owner* (KSO) for one or more key stages. The KSO accepts the obligation for his/her key stage to confirm:

- the work to be done is identified at the detailed task level:
- the dependencies are clearly identified;
- the estimates of durations are accurate and subject to constant scrutiny;
- the work gets done on time to the quality needed;
- the work conforms to quality assurance procedures and requirements;
- regular monitoring is maintained;
- regular accurate status reports are issued;
- problems and issues are alerted promptly to you.

RECORD YOUR ALLOCATED RESPONSIBILITIES

Communication document for everyone involved including the line managers of the resources assigned to the project. As the plan develops more names are added as the extended team is identified for parts of the detailed work. Your *responsibility chart* should record:

- a list of the key stages and for each;
- who is responsible;
- who should be consulted for advice;
- who must be kept informed of progress;

and later add:

- planned start date;
- planned finish date;
- whether a critical activity.

Your reason for allocating these responsibilities is to assign the estimating of key stage durations to those people in your team who are most likely to have the appropriate experience or know who to consult to get the experienced inputs.

ESTIMATING

An estimate is a decision about how much time and resources are required to carry out a piece of work to acceptable standards of performance. This requires you to determine: the 'size' of the task or group of tasks, as determined from measurements if possible; and the amount of 'effort' required to complete the work. You must ask: how can the work be broken down? and can it be divided between two or more people?

Effort is measured in project time units–hours/days/weeks. Once the effort is known then optimise the resource needs, taking individual available time into account to determine the amount of effort required from each. Effort is a direct measure of a person's time to do a piece of work in normal workdays.

Duration is a conversion of effort taking into account the number of people involved, their capacities and an allowance for non-productive time. Since duration is measured in real working days this is never the same as the schedule, which has to take into account:

- non-available days for project work;
- non-working days–weekends;
- public and organisation holidays;
- staff holidays.

The first step for you is to derive some realistic durations and then apply these to a calendar to derive a schedule.

Forecasting Durations

As the duration of each key stage is the real time it will take to complete the work this is usually the most difficult part of the planning process. *It has been demonstrated many times that the majority of projects start with a schedule that has an inherent slippage of up to 30 per cent before you start the work.* This is largely due to poor estimating. The sources for accurate estimates are limited:

- experience of others;
- the expert view;
- historical data from other projects.

There is no substitute for experience. If similar work has been done before then you can ask others for their own previous experience and adjust the data for your project. It is a reasonable way to start but always take a cautious approach. The equation relating *effort* and *performance* is different for us all.

Who are the experts? There may be a few–or so they believe! Always ask questions about how reality compared with original estimates for some work. Check that the nature or content of the work did not change. You soon discover who is above average at estimating accurately.

Contingencies

The purpose of contingencies is to attempt to quantify two additional factors:

1. The extent of uncertainty in the estimating process based on expected work content.
2. The risks associated with a particular piece of work.

Contingencies are not intended to cover changes to the project definition or objectives after they have been agreed with the stakeholders. Remember that most people include their own contingencies to protect themselves when asked for time estimates!

Agree the durations to be inserted in the plan with the team. These lead you to calculating the total project time with a projected completion date. Obviously there is a balance between the desired project completion date and the projected or forecast completion date based only on estimates. Somewhere in the middle there is an acceptable solution and only attention to detail and all the experience you can gather will help you to find it.

Time Limited Scheduling and Estimates

Imposed completion dates, given to you before any planning is carried out, always creates a conflict. This impost date forces you to compress estimates to fit the date. To a limited degree this is acceptable as a target but too often this process moves you into a totally unreal situation where you are faced with 'mission impossible'. You must still prepare realistic estimates to derive a clear case and state:

- what you can deliver in the time;
- what you cannot deliver in the time;
- why you can only meet part of the objectives of the project.

You can then use your skill as a negotiator to arrive at an agreed solution!

Guidelines for Estimating

- Schedule full time team members at 3.5–4.0 working (productive) days per week (to allow for holidays, absences, training courses, etc.)
- Include management time where appropriate as an additional 10 per cent.
- In planning, avoid splitting tasks between individuals.
- When tasks are split between two individuals do not reduce time by 50 per cent–allow time for communication and coordination.
- Take individual experience and ability into account.
- Allow time for cross-functional data transfer and responses.
- Build in time for unscheduled urgent tasks arising on other non-project activities.
- Build in spare time for problem solving and project meetings.

For each key stage keep a record of:

- the estimates you have finally decided;
- any assumptions made during estimating;
- where contingencies have been added;
- how much contingency has been added.

THE CRITICAL PATH OF YOUR PROJECT

Critical path techniques have been in use on projects now for some 30 years, having proved their value as a tool for project scheduling and control. The fundamental purpose is to enable you to find the shortest possible time in which to complete your project. You can do this by inspection of the *logic diagram.*

Enter the durations on to your notelets in the logic diagram for each key stage. Begin at the START notelet and trace each possible route or path through the diagram to the FINISH notelet, adding the durations of all the key stages in the path. The path that has the highest number, that is, the longest duration, is the 'critical path' of your project and takes the least time to complete the project. All other paths are shorter. All the key stages on the critical path must, by definition, finish on time or the project schedule will slip.

This is where reality hits you–is the project total time what your customer actually expects? If it is a long way out, do not worry yet as most project managers expect this to happen. Remember your estimates are based on people's perceptions. Your objective is to attempt to compress the schedule to a time that is both real and achievable and satisfies your customer. Fortunately another valuable tool of project management is available to help you–*programme review and evaluation technique* (PERT for short). This tool allows you to analyse the logic diagram to confirm:

- the critical path–confirmation of your initial inspection;
- the start and finish times for all the key stages;
- the amount of 'spare time' available in the non-critical key stages.

The value of this data is to give you information for optimising the project schedule. This tool also provides you with the means to control the project work once this starts.

The PERT Critical Analysis Technique

The PERT method of critical path planning and scheduling is the most commonly used technique for project management control. It is based on representing the activities in a project by boxes (or nodes) that contain essential information calculated about the project. The inter-dependencies between the activities are represented by arrows to show the flow of the project through its various paths in the logic diagram. The PERT diagram (sometimes referred to as a network) is identical to the

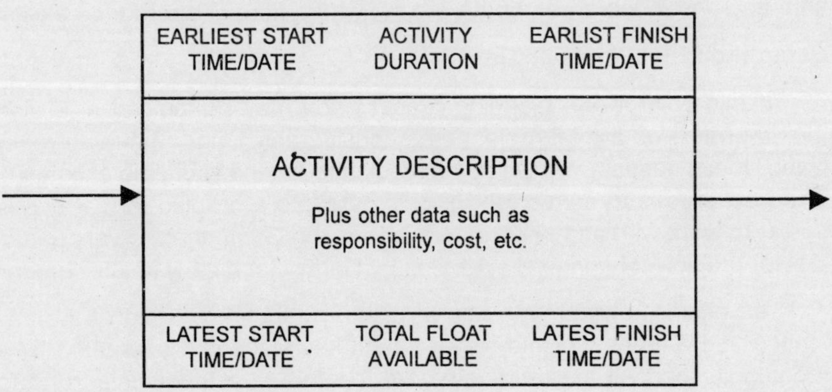

Figure 4.4: The PERT node box.

a node. The following paragraphs explain the conventional data stored in the node box.

The four corners of the node box are used to store the four characteristic times for the key stage. These are calculated times using the durations derived in estimating–remember to keep all durations in the same units.

The default or normal relationship used is FINISH to START. Under certain circumstances it is valid to impose constraints with the START to START or FINISH to FINISH relationships between activities, that is, pairs of activities are forced to start or finish together. You can impose a forced delay using a LAG between the START or FINISH of a predecessor activity and the START or FINISH of one or more successor activities. The forced start, or LEAD, is used to start a SUCCESSOR ACTIVITY before the PREDECESSOR ACTIVITY is completed.

Lags and leads should be used with care–it is easy to become confused and introduce errors. Split an activity instead of using leads, to keep the diagram relatively easy to read and understand.

Analysing the Logic Diagram

The analysis of the diagram is a simple logical process extending the initial calculation you made earlier to locate the critical path. Two steps are involved:

1. Adding durations from start to finish–the *forward pass;*
2. Subtracting the durations from finish to start–the *backward pass.*

In this way you and your team can quickly calculate the total project time and find those areas of the project where float or spare time exists.

Using the PERT Analysis Data

At this point in the planning process you may be looking at a plan that is giving you a total project time considerably longer than you really want. Do not despair–yet! Do not go back and amend your time estimates. The next step is to convert the PERT data into a graphic format this is easier to work with and understand. This is the *Gantt chart*–a very useful tool for project work originally devised by Henry Gantt early in this century.

The chart is divided into two sections, a tabulated listing of the key stages and a graphic display where each key stage is represented by a rectangular bar. All the rectangles are located on a time-scaled grid to show their position in the schedule. It is useful to have both a project time scale bar and a calendar time scale bar across the top of the chart. This allows you to include the non-working days such as weekends and holidays. The key stages are listed on the left-hand side by convention, in order of their occurrence in the logic diagram (working from left to right).

You will note that the *total float time* is also shown on the chart as a line extension to those rectangles, or bars (the common term), on the right-hand end, that is, at the finish end of the bar. When you initially draw any Gantt chart the total float is *always* drawn at this end. The limit of total float is the limit of the time available for an activity or a group of activities in series, if the schedule is not to be threatened and extend the whole project. Total float is not cumulative in the whole diagram, only on a single path.

Of course *critical activities* have zero float and you can choose to highlight these with the use of colour. You can also include the dependency arrows on the chart between the start and finish of the dependent activities (ignoring the float zone). The Gantt chart can also show some other useful information:

- Milestones–special checkpoints usually indicated by a triangle or a diamond symbol;
- Project meetings–indicated by a filled circle or dot;
- Project reviews (ie financial/audit)–indicated by a filled square;
- Key decision points–often called 'gates'.

Remember to give a egend describing what the symbols mean!

The initial Gantt chart you produce at this stage is then optimised to reflect what you can achieve with available resources balanced with customer desires. This frequently involves compressing the schedule to reduce the time for the project.

Using a Computer

The optimisation may involve considerable reiteration to arrive at an acceptable solution--a process where project management software is very powerful. Small changes in the schedule are rapidly reflected in the chart and the logic simultaneously recalculated automatically. This allows you to carry out 'what if' analysis, viewing the impact of changing anything in your plan in a host of different ways. You can explore all available options you can think of to derive a finally acceptable schedule.

This process is necessary to convince your customer and the project sponsor just what is realistically possible if clear commitments of resources are made. Obviously this process is much more time consuming manually!

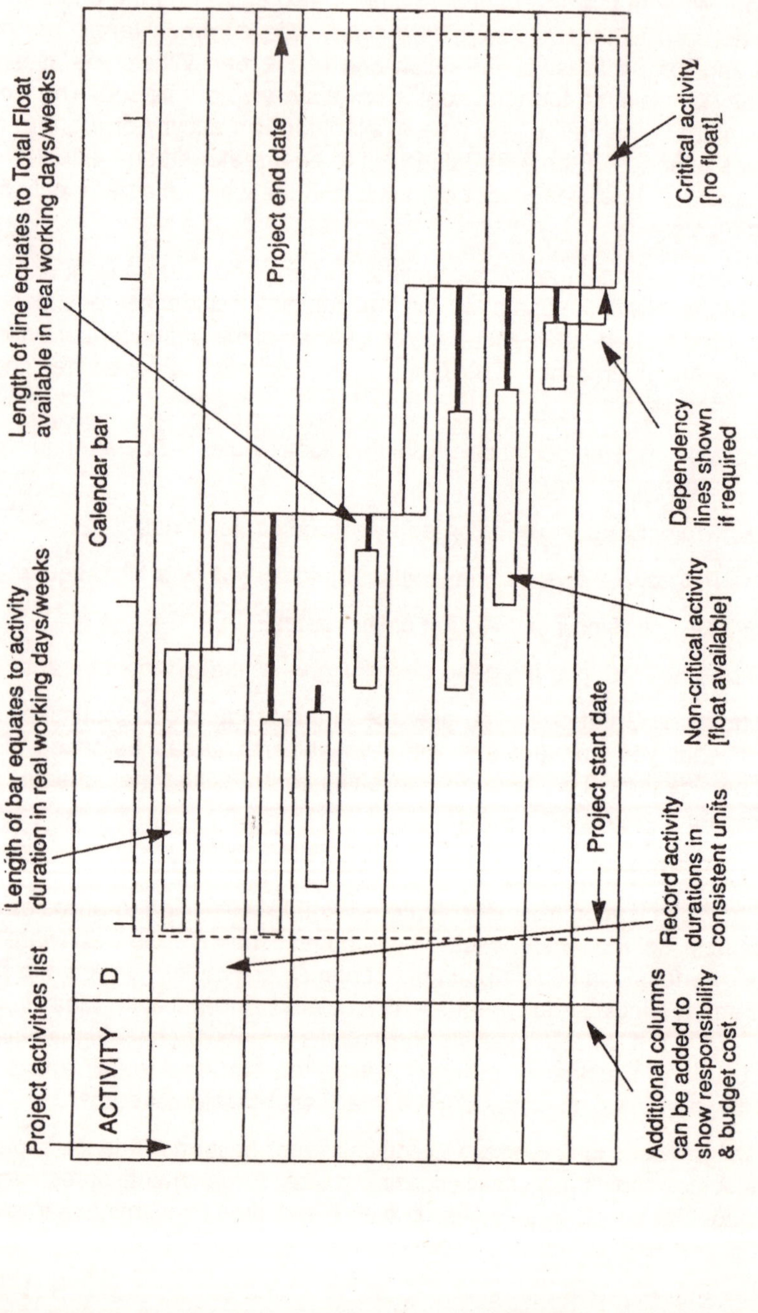

Figure 4.5: The Gants Chart Schedule

ANALYSE RESOURCE REQUIREMENTS

Ask you KSOs to validate the task list in their respective key stages using the taskboarding technique. Much of the data will have been generated earlier but this now needs some closer analysis, particularly for the initial key stages. Identify the resources most likely to be assigned the work and then working with them as an extended team:

- review the initial task list;
- add to the tasks where necessary;
- analyse for the 'often forgotten tasks':
  - documentation;
  - approval times;
  - testing planning and development;
  - project meetings, replanting and planning reviews;
  - project reviews and gathering the data;
  - customer meetings and user group meetings;
  - negotiations with suppliers;
  - expediting and administration.

Suggest each key stage owner:

- derives a complete list of tasks in their key stage;
- produces a responsibility chart for each key stage;
- estimates the durations of all the tasks in the key stage;
- identifies the actual people who will carry out the work;
- confirms their commitment and availability.

It is good practice to derive the logic diagram for all the tasks inside each key stage. Then determine the critical path and the total float available in the tasks. Some of these tasks may be assigned milestone status later. This enables you to produce a Gantt chart for each key stage. In this way a detailed plan of the work for a particular part of the project is clearly defined by the people doing the work and it minimises misunderstandings about responsibility.

An advantage of this method is that the detailed work of a key stage does not need to be derived until a few weeks before the work starts. This allows the planing to incorporate any unexpected outputs from earlier key stages. In this way you continuously work to hold your plan dates, seek the required resources, validate your estimates and optimise your schedule to meet the total project time desired.

Optimising your Schedule

The schedule is always based on the calendar, taking into account the non-working days during the project. It involves taking decisions by consensus to maintain a balance between:

- the schedule–time;
- the resources available–cost;
- performance–scope and quality.

The options available are fairly limited when optimising trade-offs between these three to arrive at a solution.

There is no perfect plan, only the best solution based on available information at the time. The options are:

- re-evaluate the dependencies in the logic for the key stages;
- review relationship–initially you used FINISH TO START, now examine if other types give an improvement;
- introduce LAGS and LEADS–with caution though;
- split key stages to get more concurrency;
- review assigned durations–review any contingencies added;
- review original estimates–realistically;
- seek more or different resources;
- seek to get current resource capacities increased–more time available;
- examine to ensure re-invention is minimised;
- reduce scope or quality or specifications–a last resort option.

When you are confident you have a realistic acceptable schedule update the key stage Gantt chart. Check your original project definition to ensure you have not ignored anything–particularly expected dates quoted and assumptions made. Present this schedule informally to your customer and project sponsor top confirm if it is acceptable. If not, then you must seek alternative solutions through further optimisation. If the schedule is nominally agreed you can proceed to the final steps of planning before launching the actual work.

REVIEW THE PROJECT RISK LOG

Review all the risks identified during the project definition phase. Ask:

- Have any changed status?
- Are there any new HIGH risks?
- Are there any new risks identified from planning?
- Examine your schedule top identify possible risks:
  - tasks on the critical path (and inside a key stage);
  - tasks with a long duration (low capacity factors?);
  - tasks succeeding a merge of two or more activities;
  - tasks with little float left (where is the float?);
  - tasks dependent on third parties;
  - lags and leads;
  - start to start relationships;
  - tasks using several people;
  - complex tasks;
  - anything involving a steep learning curve;
  - tasks using new or unproved technology.

Prepare new action plans for any new HIGH risks identified or those that have moved up in ranking. Assign responsibilities for day to day monitoring of risks to the KSOs. Avoiding a risk is better than a damage limitation exercise later!

REVIEW THE PROJECT BUDGET

Begin by updating the project WBS with all the lower level detail–or at least as much as you can at this stage. This is the easiest way to work out the cost of each based on:

- capital equipment costs;
- resource direct costs-based on cost rates;
- revenue costs for the project team;
- indirect costs–chargeable overheads, etc.

With the costs of each key stage identified you can produce an *operating budget* – the real budget for project control purposes. If it varies significantly to the original *approved budget* in the business case then this variance must be investigated and the conflict resolved. If an increased cost is identified then the customer will need to be consulted for approval. Prepare for this discussion by deriving some alternate options as you did when optimising the schedule earlier. Keep a record of all costs for control measurement and variance analysis.

FREEZING THE BASELINE SCHEDULE

Review the schedule you have now derived and make sure you have not forgotten anything! This is soon to be frozen as the baseline schedule. Everything that happens in future will be measured against this schedule. You will need to present the plan documents to your sponsor and then the customer for approval and acceptance. Use this checklist to review the plans with the team and ensure you have not forgotten anything:

- Is the project definition still completely valid?
- Is the scope of work statement still valid?
- Has the project manager's authority been confirmed in writing?
- Are all stakeholders identified?
- Does the team understand who manages the stakeholders?
- Is the WBS developed as far as practicable?
- Does the WBS include all administration tasks?
- Are customer and sign-off checkpoint meetings included?
- Is the current critical path established and agreed?
- Are all key stages allocated for responsibility?
- Are KSOs clear about their responsibilities?
- Is the project risk log complete and up to date?
- Are duration estimations recorded?
- Are resource loadings and capacities optimised and agreed?
- Does the Gantt chart reflect an agreed schedule?
- Has the project operating budget been approved?
- Have supporting plans (as required) been derived for quality assurance, communication, configuration management?
- Does the team include all the skills needed?

- Has action been taken to acquire unavailable skills needed for the project?
- Are the team members working well together?
- Have any conflicts been resolved promptly?

Seeking Approval to Launch

You have now completed the planning phase as far as necessary before launching the project work. At this point plan documentation comprises:

- a list of key stages;
- the project logic diagram;
- a project key stage responsibility chart;
- responsibility charts, if appropriate, for each key stage;
- a record of estimates for all the key stages;
- an optimised project Gantt chart for the key stages;
- Gantt charts for the early key stages or all of them;
- an updated and reviewed project risk log;
- a project operating budget;
- other plan documents as required.

Now present these documents to your customer and project sponsor for signature of approval to proceed, opening the gate into the next phase, launching the actual project execution.

5

Launching and Executing the Project

There are still a few things to think about before you hit the 'GO' button and launch into execution of the work. You need to validate all those promises of resource availability and confirm the reporting and communication processes.

PREPARING FOR PROJECT EXECUTION

Confirming Resource Commitments

Create the initial work plans by asking the key stage owners (KSOs) to verify their task lists, making sure they have not forgotten any tasks. You can use a standard format to record these task lists with a clear identification who is responsible for completing each task in the key stage. It is useful to also record:

- the key stage code as recorded on the WBS;
- the key stage schedule start and end dates, whether it is critical and calculated float;
- the duration of each task in the key stage using consistent units;
- the amount of float in each task if this has been calculated;
- the plan START and END dates for each task;
- a record of the ACTUAL START and END dates for each task.

Copy and send the work plans produced to the people involved and their line managers. This reminds them of the contract they have concluded. The original estimates of duration are only as good as the information available at the time.

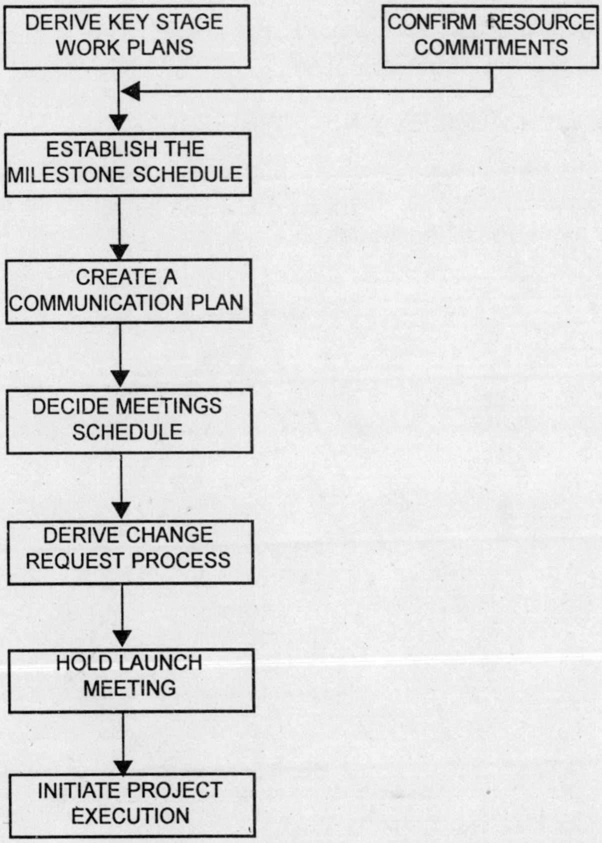

Figure 5.1 The Launch Process.

If the result is not acceptable revisit your schedule and if appropriate optimise the schedule using the same approach as before. Your choices are limited but usually enough to come up with a satisfactory and acceptable solution:

- seek more resource capacity;
- obtain more resources;
- review and modify the logic inside the key stage;
- amend the scope or quality of the work.

Although this may seem to be a time consuming activity, you are only asking your team to use a consistent and disciplined approach to work planning. You do not need to produce all the work plans at the outset, just those for the first few key states. As the project continues, you can work proactively to prepare more work plans, taking into full account everything that has happened in the project. This is known as 'layering the plan' as the project proceeds.

ESTABLISH A MILESTONE SCHEDULE

Earlier we showed how risks and issues relate to the project schedule; The *milestones* are an integral part of this schedule so they are subject to the same risks and issues:

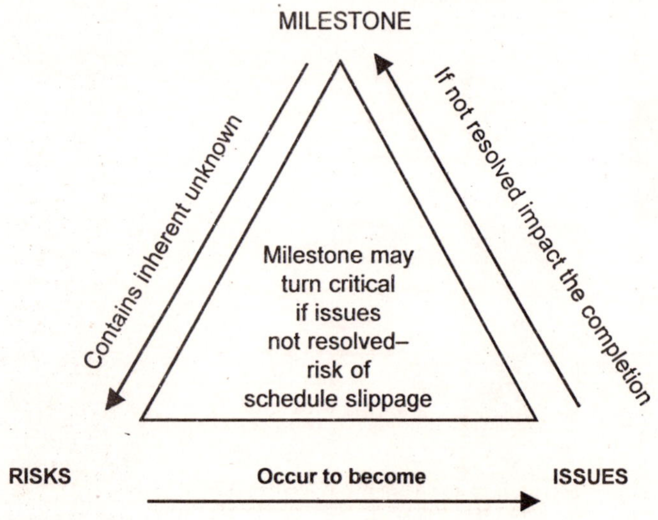

Figure 5.2: Milestone and Risks.

The milestones are all the significant events that are due to occur during the execution of the project. The milestone is a flag or signal at some clearly defined point in the project. The milestone is a point of control, placing target points in the project schedule for certain events to be signed off as completed. Milestones are either 100 per cent complete or not complete - there is not partial completion!

Some of the common events given the status of project milestones are:

- completion of a key task, for example, providing output to third parties;
- completion of one of the project deliverables;
- stage generation of benefits;

- completion of a third party significant event, for example, acceptance tests;
- completion of third party activity, for example, delivery of equipment or data;
- a financial audit point;
- a project audit point;
- a quality audit;
- completion of a significant stage of work (possibly a critical element);
- a significant decision point, for example, abort the project;
- completion of a project stage to release further funding.

The frequency of milestones in a network must be sufficient for effective control. Record the milestones on a schedule listing and on the Gantt chart. For effective control ALL milestones must be measurable with clearly established metrics - apply the SMART test you applied to deliverables earlier.

HAVE A COMMUNICATION PLAN

Poor communication is a major source of conflict so give this serious attention before you start the project work. Ask yourself:

- who needs to know;
- what do they need to know;
- how much do they need to know;
- how often must they be informed.

Establish distribution list(s) as appropriate but avoid generating large volumes of paper. Decide the ground rules you will impose on everyone to get prompt feedback of the prevailing situation with the work in progress. Effective monitoring and tracking of the project is dependent on good communication in the team, between you and the team and your key stakeholders. You need prompt feedback about:

- current progress of the active tasks;
- problems encountered with the work;
- problems anticipated with work waiting to be done;
- technical difficulties being encountered.

Project Status Reports

Your key stakeholders expect to receive regular status reports. Decide the frequency and format of these with your customer and sponsor. Clearly define any metrics you will use and decide just what data you need to receive about the status of the project, such as:

- what has been completed;
- what has not been completed and why;
- what is being done about the incomplete work;
- what problems remain unsolved;
- what needs to be done about these unsolved problems and when;
- what difficulties are anticipated in the work waiting to be done.

This template should at least record:

- a concise summary of overall progress;
- a list of milestones due to be completed since the last report and their current status, ie on time or late;
- a list of milestones with dates due in the next reporting period;
- actions set in place to correct any slipped milestones;
- forecasts for the project completion based on current information;
- reasons for any revision to earlier forecasts to completion;
- changes to the project risk log;
- any issues (problems) outstanding still waiting for resolution;
- costs to date compared to the budget.

No one likes to hear bad news, but the sooner it is exposed the quicker you can react to limit the damages and take corrective action. You can use this template at any level in the project - the KSOs reporting to you and your reports to the customer and sponsor. Good teamwork is directly related to effective and regular communication.

What Meetings do I Need?

The different meetings you may need include:

- one to one meetings with the project sponsor;
- one to one meetings with your team members;
- project progress meetings with the team;

- problem solving meetings;
- meetings with particular stakeholders - the customers;
- project review meetings with other stakeholders.

All are necessary at different frequencies throughout the project and all must have a clear purpose. The one to one meetings are very important to maintain close contact with your project sponsor and the members of your team helping you to:

- know and understand these people as individuals;
- give and receive information at a personal level;
- discuss problems of a more personal nature that impact on performance;
- give guidance and support;
- coach team members;
- recognise their efforts;
- encourage and support personal development.

Problem solving meetings tend to be held as problems arise, involving specific people, which may not mean the whole team. Do not mix problem solving with progress or team meetings as the discussion easily gets out of control and the meeting becomes diverted from the purpose.

Agree a schedule of project progress meetings, throughout the whole project, showing the schedule dates on the key stage Gantt chart. If you have nothing to discuss, cancel or postpone any meeting.

HANDLING PROJECT CHANGES

However good your plans, there are certain to be some unexpected surprises. Minor changes appear during monitoring and are controlled by prompt reaction and taking corrective measures. Significant change is much more serious and needs closer scrutiny. These changes can come from:

- the customer;
- the end user;
- the sponsor;
- technical problems.

All can lead to replanning of the project and scope changes. Any change that is expected to create a replanning activity and affect the total project time as currently scheduled must be handled in a formal manner. Always examine:

- the source of the change request;
- why is it necessary;
- the benefits from making the change;
- the consequences of doing nothing at this stage;
- the cost impact of making the change;
- the effect on project constraints;
- the effect on resource needs;
- the increase or decrease in project risks;
- the effect on the objectives and scope of the project.

Major change can have a demotivating effect on the team unless it is something they have sought in the interests of the project. A major change on one project could have serious impact on the resource availability for another project.

Derive alternative solutions and examine the consequences and risks before seeking an agreement with the customer. Formalise change requests - this often makes many requests for changes suddenly disappear!

HOLD A LAUNCH MEETING

Now you can launch the project. The launch meeting is a milestone in your project after which all project work starts. Collect together all the important people who are involved with your project and explain the plans in some detail. Prepare yourself and your team well for the meeting. This is an important opportunity for you to explain the plan and the areas of high risk to achieving success. You are looking for acceptance from all those present that the project is well planned. You must convince them that with their cooperation you can achieve the objectives. No one can later complain they do not understand the project plan or what you are trying to achieve.

Maintaining Plan Integrity

New information inevitably comes in to the team members after the work starts. This can be quite casual through informal meetings in the corridor, staff restaurant or even the car park, or through lower level sources in the customer's organisation. The input is also intentional on occasions and could have profound effects on the work, the schedule and team motivation.

You must prevent any input amending the plans, increasing the scope or creating more work than necessary and remind team members to inform you immediately of such situations. You are asking your team to keep you informed of progress, so when additional information appears you (and the team members) must ask:

- Where does the information come from?
- Why was it not exposed before?
- Who has decided it is relevant now?
- Is the information accurate and realistic?
- Is there some hidden agenda associated with the timing?
- What impact does it have on the plan and schedule?
- Does this change the project objectives, deliverables or benefits?

Project work can be seriously constrained, or even sabotaged by the subtle transfer of erroneous information to a team member. A complete absence of information when it is due to appear can have similar sinister origins. Always be openly prepared to consider changes to your plan when essential. If the information and data essential to the project work is confused by mixed messages from different people then you face potential conflicts and confusion. Prepare your team for these events because they are certain to occur at some time in the project's life - if you have nor experienced them already! Establish an early warning system to ensure you get rapid feedback about what has happened and what needs to happen. This provides you with the information to control the project.

THE CONTROL ENVIRONMENT

Control of a project environment involves three operating modes:

- *measuring* - determining progress by formal and informal reporting;
- *evaluating* - determining cause of deviations from the plan;
- *correcting* - taking actions to correct.

Control is associated with the present, so reporting is time-sensitive to allow you to take prompt corrective action.

The communication processes you established during the project launch are designed to give on-time visibility to significant events.

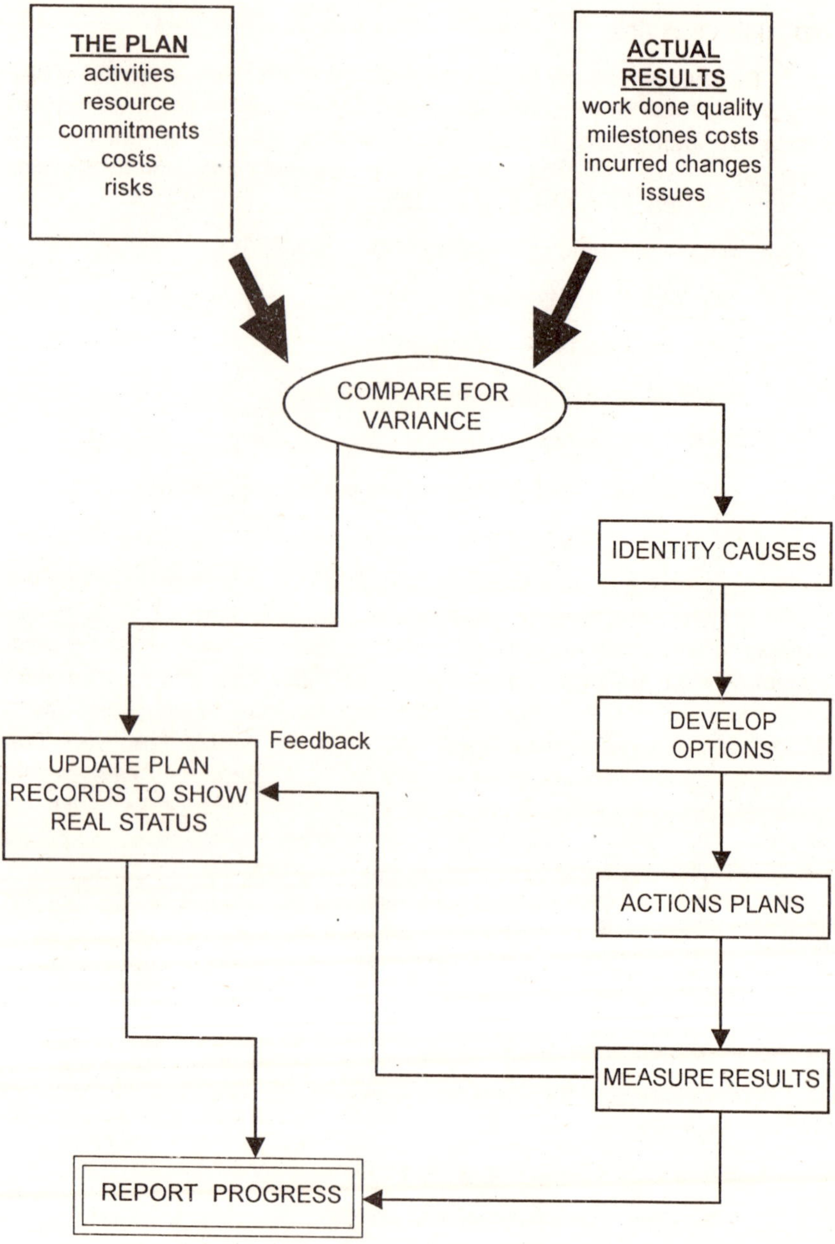

Fig. 5.3: The Project Control System

Design Your Control System

The purpose is to ensure that you and the team always have the information to make an accurate assessment of progress and keep the project under control

The best control system is the simplest. The basic inputs to control are the schedule and the actual results observed and measured by the team. The comparison activity should show whether the project is on track and everything is going according to plan. If this is true you can update the project records and charts and report progress and any slippage to your customer and project sponsor.

Corrective action plans are of no value unless you give particular attention to follow up and checking that actions have been completed and produced the desired result. Controlling the project means managing the many problems that arise to maintain the project baseline schedule through:

- monitoring the work - observing and checking what is happening;
- identifying and resolving the issues that arise:
- tracking the project - comparing with the plan and updating the records.

Remind them that the total float is not spare time for them to use as they like without reference to you. Keep the project records up to date with a regular check and update of:

- the organisation chart;
- the stakeholder list;
- the key stage responsibility charts;
- the key stage Gantt chart;
- the work plans;
- the project risk log;
- the project issue log.

Using a project management software package can help you maintain your project data - once you are familiar with its many features!

Keeping the project records up to date is an obligation you must fulfil. You could be moved to another project at any time and someone else has to take over. Do ensure that the legacy you leave behind is a good one, otherwise you will continually be subject to queries and requests that interfere with your new role.

MONITORING THE PROGRESS

This is not done by waiting for progress reports to be issued. You need to walk about, observe and have conversations! This is your data gathering process, which if done effectively is far more useful then any written report. Confidence in progress reports only comes from verifying these from time to time. This obliges you to monitor both the team performance and the stakeholders' performance. Monitoring is a checking activity to:

- talk to the team members to find out directly how things are going;
- encourage the team and show you care about them and their work;
- check that promised resources are in fact working on project tasks;
- rapidly learn about concerns and difficulties.

Excessive monitoring may be perceived as interference, so there is a fine balance between the two extremes.

Measuring the Progress

Ask the team how progress is easily measured. They must agree:

- the output criteria for each activity;
- the performance metrics to use and confirm completion;
- the frequency of measuring and recording;
- how to report the progress deviations or exceptions.

If unusual or unexpected results appear you need to be informed promptly so that corrective action can be decided. Remind the team to watch out for the risks that are particularly relevant at each stage of the work - these can produce real roadblocks.

Managing the Issues Arising

The purpose of an *issue management process* is to make sure all risks that happen are resolved promptly to avoid and/or limit damage to your project. Generally issues do not go away and success depends on this prompt action.

Managing issues is similar to managing the original risks, requiring you to keep records of all issues that occur, and ensure action planning is promptly used to resolve the issues. Your concern must be to get an

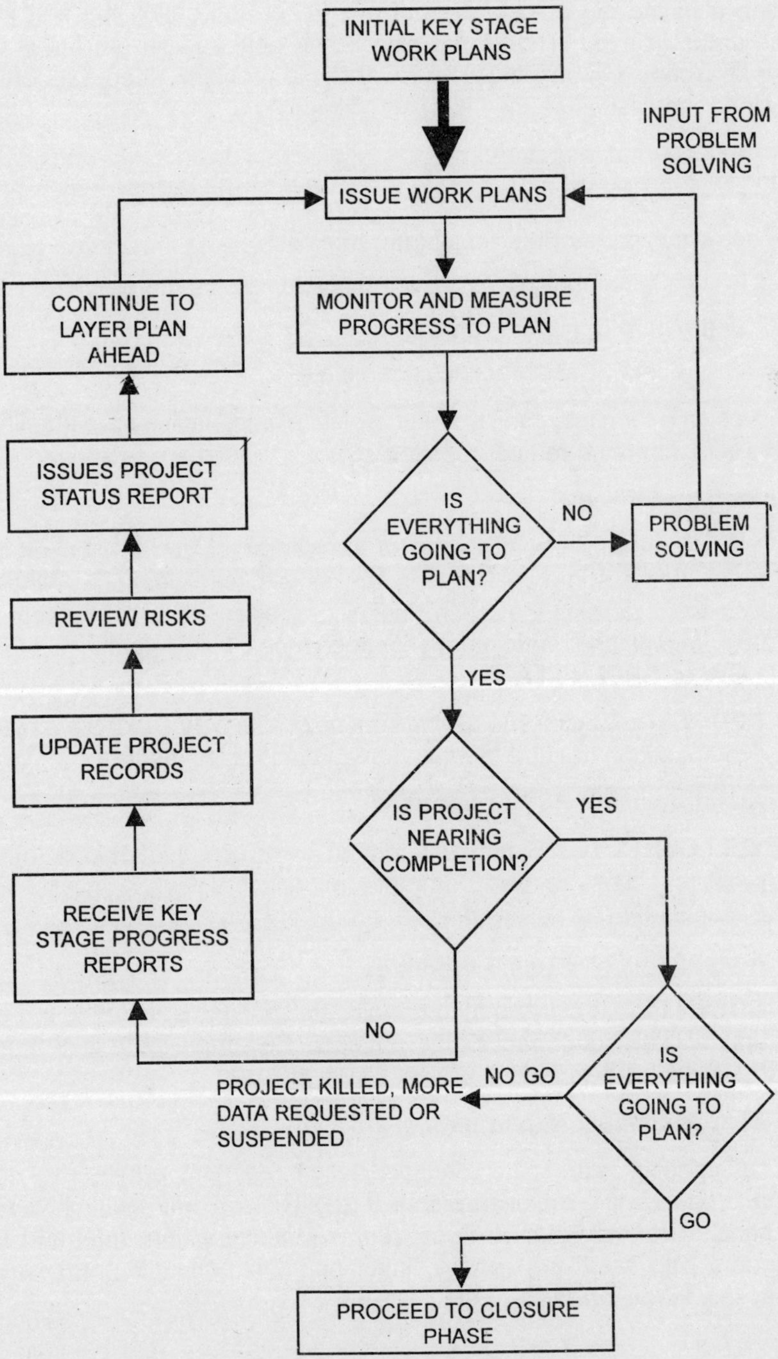

Figure 5.4: The Monitroring Process

action plan moving quickly. Do not over-react and action the first idea that jumps to mind. This is not always the best solution so utilise the team's expertise in deriving an answer to the problem. Keep a record of all significant issues as they happen giving:

- issue name and source;
- who owns it for resolution;
- which parts of the project are affected;
- who is responsible for action plans to resolve the problem;
- a record of current ranking;
- a record of when action is complete.

Design a template similar to the project risk log. Issues are identified and tracked through regular monitoring.

Ranking the Issues

You will probably resolve must of the issues but some will need the authority of the sponsor. Ranking an issue clearly identifies who is responsible for deriving the action plan. Issues raised are ranked according to their impact and anticipated consequences by assigning a RED, YELLOW or GREEN FLAG.

RED FLAG: Major issue having serious consequences for the project. Prompt action needed to implement a decision to resolve.

***Responsibility:* PST or sponsor**

YELLOW FLAG: Significant impact on the project and/or other projects. Unless resolved promptly will cause delays to milestones. Becomes **RED** if action delayed more than two or three days.

***Responsibility*: Project sponsor**

GREEN FLAG: Consequences limited to confined area of the project and unlikely to impact other projects. Becomes **YELLOW** if not resolved in time to avoid project slippage.

Responsibility*: *Project manager

Outstanding issues are identified when reporting progress of the project. You must also ensure that the ranking of any issue has not changed. It is important to keep your key stakeholders informed on progress with resolving issues, invoking their active support when necessary in the interests of the project.

Resolving Issues

Remember it is the issues that are the 'success killers' interfering with your target of maintaining the project schedule so apart from prompt reaction, ensure you:

- involve the team in solving problems;
- use additional expertise where appropriate;
- identify areas of the project affected:
  - consequences as perceived now;
  - consequences in the future if not resolved;
  - options to resolve the problem and for each option:
  - cost and resource implications;
  - effects on the project schedule;
  - effects on scope – quality;
  - risks associated and new risks created;
  - future issues identified/uncovered.

Always confirm that responsibility is clearly allocated for actions:

- Who is responsible?
- When must the action be completed?
- Who must be kept informed of progress?
- Who monitors - during and after?

TRACKING YOUR PROJECT

Tracking is the process by which the project progress is measured through monitoring to ensure that changes to the schedule caused by issues or the customer are promptly acted upon and that the reported progress data is used to update the plan charts and records in the project file.

Your starting point is the baseline against which the variances are identified. The baseline for all tracking is the project baseline schedule and other plan documents devised and frozen before implementation, when all key stages are fixed. The project baseline should remain unchanged throughout the project. As the work is done you mark progress on the chart by filling in the bars to show the amount of work completed.

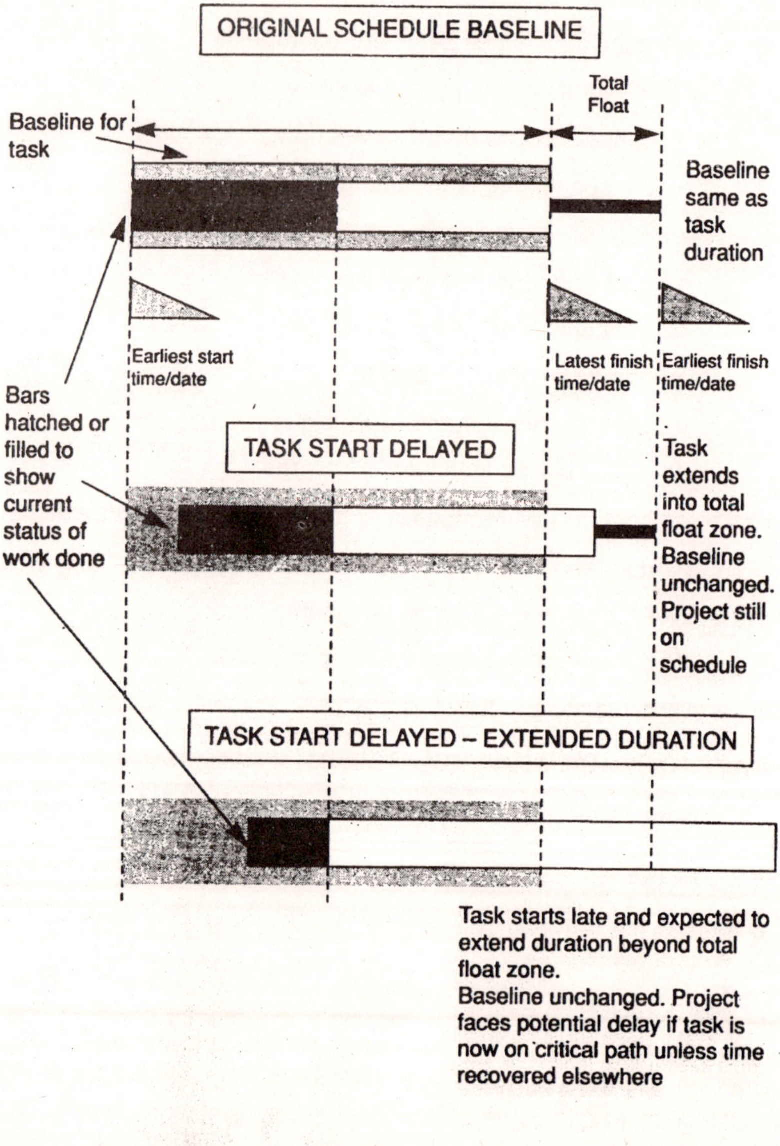

Figure 5.5: Progress on the Grant Chart

If a key stage is late starting, takes longer to complete, or the finish suffers a delay, this is shown clearly on the chart. The original position of the bar on the chart is unchanged as the baseline. Modifications to the schedule are recorded as they occur to enable the experience to be logged for future projects. This may move one or more activities away from the original baseline position, modifying the project strategy for a reason. Keeping the baseline unchanged forces you to fully document any changes to the plan and schedule and later evaluate the key learning points from all these changes that occur.

If any of these modifications cause a slippage to critical key stages then the project completion will be delayed. You then face the difficult task of recovery planning to restore the original project schedule or persuade the customer to accept the extended completion date. Serious slippage of non-critical activities may turn them critical, leading to a new critical path for the project. The critical path is never fixed unless everything happens exactly as scheduled.

Define Completion

Clearly define what everyone understands by completion. The bar on a schedule is a linear graphical representation of effort. In real life, effort is never linear and depends on:

- the accuracy of the detailed planning of tasks to do;
- the complexity of the work;
- the amount of interruptions to the work;
- the availability of data and equipment;
- how the individual feels on the day.

Per cent complete assessments are often quoted in progress reports. These are of little value and you need to know whether the task will finish in time, so ask for a forecast of when it will be completed. This focuses the individual responsible for the work to review other commitments due in the same period and give a more realistic assessment of the time to complete. If the forecast completion date is then clearly unacceptable, take some prompt corrective action. Persuade all your KSOs to get into the habit of forecasting performance for their key stages.

Ensure the progress reports give reasons for any changes to previous forecast completion dates. Encourage the team to develop expertise in accurate forecasting to expose potential future variances. The analysis for variances at all stages must be a primary concern for the whole team, making sure effective corrective action is taken when any issues occur.

Analysis of a variance is essential to expose the causes of the problem. Your primary concern is to maintain schedule integrity - no slippages. Taking corrective action usually has limited possibilities:

- rearrange workload(s) if a milestone date is going to be missed;
- put more effort into the job;
- put additional resources on to the job;
- move the milestone date;
- lower the scope and/or quality of the results demanded by the plan.

Corrective action is normally approached using these options in this order, remembering all could have a cost implication. Record any assumptions you make when deciding action plans - they could have significance later! Before deciding action plans check if:

- the critical path has changed;
- any individual workloads are adversely affected;
- any other milestones are subject to slippage;
- any new HIGH risks are exposed;
- any new ISSUES are exposed.
- any cost over-runs are introduced - do these need approval;
- any localised schedule slippages are controllable.

Progress Reporting

Check with your customer and the project sponsor that they are getting all the essential information they need. Avoid creating an enormous paper trail. Keep reports short using templates, but expect to make a more detailed presentation occasionally at a full project review. Focus the reports on the project milestones:

- short summary of progress;
- milestones due and completed;
- milestones due that have slipped;
- corrective actions put in place to recover the slippage;
- milestones due in next reporting period;
- issues cscalated and waiting for decisions;

- new issues escalated to sponsor or PST;
- forecast of project completion date;
- forecast of project cost at completion;
- any significant changes requested and actions proposed/taken;
- reasons for any revision of previous forecasts.

Project control is dependent on good communication and feedback. Keep the process working to avoid confusion and misunderstandings and ensure all your project records are up to date.

Progress Meetings

Everyone hates meetings but regular progress meetings are an important part of the project control process to review the current status at any time. Take specific actions to make them effective. Everything that has happened before the meeting is ancient history! Remember that time spent in a meeting is time lost to project work, so:

- keep your progress meetings short - maximum one hour;
- keep meetings to the point and focused on exceptions;
- avoid diversions and problem solving;
- start and finish on time;
- maintain good control;
- have the updated key stage Gantt chart available for reference;
- identify the outstanding issues but do not try to solve them in the meeting - set up a separate discussion with the relevant people.

Focus the team to expose:

- what has been completed on time;
- any outstanding exceptions to the work done;
- what actions agreed earlier are incomplete;
- when outstanding action plans will be complete;
- which milestones are completed on time;
- which milestones have slipped;
- whether action plans are in place to correct slippages;
- any risks escalated to issues;

- issues still waiting to be resolved;
- any resource capacity changes forecast;
- what work is to be done in the next period;
- which milestones are due in the next period;
- what problems are anticipated in the next period;
- any risks that could affect the work in the next period;
- any problems anticipated with third party contracts in the next period.
- any team performance problems and issues;
- whether the business case is still valid.

Always have a flip chart in the meeting room and record agreed actions on the sheet as they occur with responsibility and target completion date. In this way there should be no doubt in the team who is responsible for which actions and they do not have to wait for the minutes. Avoid:

- long verbal reports of what has been done;
- problem solving in the meeting - take serious issues off-line;
- long debates - they detract from the purpose and cause deviation;
- negotiations - usually excludes most of those present;
- 'any other business' - the biggest timewaster!

CONTROL THE COSTS

The best way to control your project is to focus on cost measurement. To demonstrate success you must not exceed the budget.

Accurate cost control is only effective if *all* costs are measured, including the costs of people working on the project. This means everyone must record their time spent on project work so that this can be costed. Cost rates often include all indirect costs such as rents, heating, lighting, etc. for the organisation. If the time data is not collected in a consistent and disciplined way, then you cannot control the costs very accurately. Your monitoring process must, therefore, include accurate measurement of:

- the time spent on each task;
- the resources used on all tasks;
- cost of materials (and wastage) used;

- cost of equipment time used;
- capital expenditure committed;
- revenue expenditure committed.

Normally these measurements are made over a specific period of two or four weeks or by calendar month. Alternatively you must resort to applying cost rates to the planned resource allocations. This assumes that what actually happens is exactly as planned. As we know this is not true, you must adjust the costs for each activity based on actual start and finish dates.

For effective control you need information on:

- the project budget as fixed in the business case;
- the project operating budget, a cumulative total based on the WBS;
- the costs incurred in the current accounting period;
- the costs incurred to date from the start;
- the work scheduled for completion according to the schedule in the current period;
- the total work scheduled for completion to date;
- the work actually completed in the current period;
- the total work actually completed to date.

The work breakdown structure is the essential budget building tool to derive an operating budget. Then measure costs incurred as the work proceeds and compare with this budget.

Cost Control Measures

Four essential measures are used for the control of project costs:

BAC - budget at completion: this is based on the operating budget developed from the WBS for the whole project.

BCWS - budgeted cost of the work scheduled: at any specific time the schedule shows a certain amount of work should be completed. This is presented as a percentage completion of the total work of the project at that time. Then:

% Scheduled Completion × BAC = BCWS

BCWP - budgeted cost of the work performed: at any specified time the actual work measured as complete is compared with the scheduled amount and the real percentage completion calculated. Then:

$$\% \text{ Actual Completion} \times BAC = BCWP$$

The BCWP is the earned value of the work of the work completed.

ACWP - actual cost of work performed: at any specified time the actual cost incurred for the work. The timing of the actual cost measurement coincides with the percentages completion progress measurement so that the actual cost can be compared with earned value (BCWP).

Other terms often used include:

FTC - forecast to complete: a forecast of the cost to be incurred to complete the remaining work. This may be an extrapolation using an analysis model or simply the best estimates of all the costs to complete the project.

CV - cost variance: the difference between the value of the work performed and the actual cost for that work, that is:

$$CV = BCWP - ACWP$$

If the actual cost is above budget the CV becomes negative!

SV - schedule variance: the difference between the value of the work performed and the value of the work that had been scheduled to be performed, at the same measurement point in time, that is:

$$SV = BCWP - BCWS$$

If the work done is behind schedule the SV becomes negative!

The variance measures are often used for trend analysis, because of their sensitivity to changes as the project progresses.

Recording Cost Data

The simplest way is to tabulate all data using a spreadsheet on a computer to calculate and update the data at regular intervals. Alternatively most project management software includes these standard cost control measures. This makes it easier to incorporate any amendments to the budget resulting from major changes to the project. Most spreadsheets and project software include charting features and the data is then used to automatically generate a chart showing the progress of the BCWP, and ACWP against the BCWS as the project progresses. Keeping your own records of costs also ensures it is regularly updated. It provides you with real-time data to compare with financial budget reports issued from other sources.

6

Secrets of Success

The biggest secret of success lies in your attitude toward your work. To be successful you need to have a positive attitude. You have to think how to solve even the most critical problems and how to come out of even the worst situations. It is basically this approach which distinguishes the successful people from others. Unlike the latter, people with positive approach never start counting the difficulties, the hurdles and the problems they may face in taking up a particular task. That's the way the successful people think. One must endeavour to take risks, at least calculated risks. To-be-or-not-to-be kind of attitude is not going to lead you anywhere or do you any good. You are in the field, come, play like a good sportsman. Kick the ball and start the game!

SUCCESS FITS WELL INTO VLCC

The owner of VLCC, one of the largely acclaimed fitness centres of India, Mrs. Vandana Luthra a housewife turned entrepreneur, sees curls and curves in the road to success. Some twelve years ago, with a small parlour at Safdarjung Enclave, Mrs. Luthra kick-started her entrepreneurial debut. Success began to grace her when she first roped in the franchisees with her then novel scheme "Goodwill understanding". Her 60:40 profit sharing formula did attract a lot many entrepreneurs then. Thereafter she succeeded in setting up some 10 centres in Delhi and more than 20 all over the country today.

SADHANA'S INSPIRATION

To this 46 year old president of Country Inn Hotels and Resorts–a group of Usha enterprise, although it is a must to maintain good rapport with your staff, a command over them would always give you advantage. Her rise from a traditional '*bahu*' of a Marwari orthodox family to a sophisticated and successful entrepreneur could be an inspiration for those aspiring members of the fairer sex who have a zeal for achieving excellency in the entrepreneurship.

AMBANI'S GREATEST STRENGTH

Most of the successful businessmen or industrialists had their dreams which they materialised. We have the classic rags to riches story of Dhirubhai Hirachand Ambani, Reliance Textiles, a school teacher's son, who initially started his entrepreneurial venture with just Rs. 15,000. The secret of success of Dhirubhai Ambani is that "he has numerous strengths as a businessman, combining a talent for everything from marketing to finance and choice of technology. If he excelled in his early years in spotting a quick money commercial opportunity, he has other strengths as well: spotting the right technology to adopt, working out innovative ways of marketing his yarn and financial wizardry with the hallmark of genius that has not been seen in Indian industry for some decades. When all is said and done however, Ambani's greatest strength is probably his ability to keep adapting to the situation that comes his way in which he finds himself. As he puts, "I will go in whatever direction suits me."

That successful businessmen are not born but made or rather they make their business a great success mostly on their own efforts alone is evident from the success stories of numerous businessmen.

PENNING LUXOR'S SUCCESS STORY

Disenchanted with the quality of pens in the market, and the flood of expensive smuggled ones in the Indian market, D.K. Jain, a young entrepreneur, in 1956, ventured to fill the gap by launching a company that would provide quality and inexpensive writing instruments to one and all. In the beginning it was a hand to mouth existence, with each working day following a working night. Burning with the desire to succeed in his mission the teething problems were valiantly overcome and Luxor today has come a long way. With the 51 crore domestic market and the exports targeted at a 10 crore mark, Luxor is deemed to become an international brand, with ship loads of pens already sold to England, France, Germany and Switzerland and the Russian and the Australian markets being targeted for the same.

SPECTACULAR BUSINESS WITH SIMPLE PRODUCT

Look and behold, "an insignificant farmer's son takes on the biggest multinational in the country and becomes a multimillionaire in next to no time, with investments worth over Rs. 50 crore. The man who did the impossible–Karsanbahi Patel–is as home-grown a genius as you can get anywhere. And, in an era of fancy management jargon, he has shown what can be achieved with a simple product and a simple idea. Karsanbhai Patel worked as a chemist in Ahmedabad on a meagre salary of Rs. 450/-. He tried his hand to produce a cheat detergent and finally succeeded. Today, the detergent 'Nirma' named after his daughter, is a household name."

PAN PARAG'S SUCCESS FORMULA

It is in fact the spirit of enterprise and strong will to succeed which makes a great difference although factors for success in business may vary in different cases. The story of a street corner *bidi* salesman, M.M. Kothari is also an eye-opener. "Once his son gave the idea to sell pan masala and his wife got the formula from their landlord in Kanpur, there was no looking back. As it stands today the sale in in multi-crore figures.

With an investment of Rs. 12,000/-, Kothari launched Pan Parag. Kothari's meteoric rise owes itself to luck as much as to business acumen. Businessmen like Kothari know how to run lean organisations, keeping costs down and simplify the marketing to a level where the business runs itself."

TURNING ADVERSITY INTO PROSPERITY!

Few have the guts to turn their adversity into prosperity. Anju Modi who would have joined the ranks of lakhs of 'unfortunate' women forced by circumstances to find for themselves, had she not decided to take her adversity after marriage to join as a sales girl. Later she took up designing though she had no formal training and with her own skills and efforts became one of the best designers in the country.

FROM HIRED FURNITURE OF HCL HEIGHT!

There are innumerable instances where even well-placed persons opted out of the well-paid secured jobs and took the risk of starting their own business. One such case is of Shiv Nadar, the main force behind HCL (Hindustan Computers Ltd.). "Shiv Nadar was marketing manager in India's pioneering computer firm: DCM Data Products. Nadar, then 30 years old, decided he could make a better go of the business on his own and, along with five others in DCM, walked out one fine morning to set up their own little shop called Hindustan Computer Limited (HCL). Six bright young people, led by Shiv Nadar, quit their jobs in 1975 and pooled their money. With loans from their provident fund accounts, they managed to put together Rs. 1.75 lakhs to enter the brave new world of computers. They started with hired furniture." And the heights to which this company has reached is there for all of us to see.

WORK AND WORK

From a small shoe store named Pal Boot House located in Karnal (Haryana) to a multi-crore company, the Liberty Shoes makes an inspiring success story. The secret of their success is "Work, and work."

THE FORCE BEHIND BPL FORTE

It was 1961 when NRI, TPG Nambiar came back to his hometown Palakkad throwing up a cushy job in England. Few could imagine that this windswept town would ever host one of India's prominent electronic companies—BPL. With Nambiar setting up BPL Limited in 1963, he virtually kick-started an electronic revolution. He coupled his visionary jest with some shrewd business *manoeuvres* and with 'sheer sweat of the brow' he built this enviable electronic empire. Nambiar trekked a long way from that November of '62 when he secured a license to make electrician and test-measuring equipment. Over the years, he earned a name for his acumen, having steered BPL with a deft hand across a diverse product list. This includes computers, communications, components, instrumentation, office automation, consumer electronics, home appliances and refrigeration.

NIRULA'S NOVELTY

Nirulas, New Delhi, started their business in 1934 by setting up Hotel India, in Connaught Place and has today expanded to several branches. The main thrust of the success achieved by Nirula's was due to earning distinction in quality of eatables and service to customers and giving due consideration to the suggestions from the customers. The lesson to be drawn from their way of functioning is that one has to be very clear in one's concept of functioning. You must first visualise, like a film director the scene to be shot, the kind of scene you want to present about your business or organisation and then execute it in such a way that your imagination comes alive before the world.

MARUTI'S ROAD TO SUCCESS

The road leading to this milestone i.e. rolling out of millionth car, has not been without its share of potholes. Recalling his early years, R.C. Bhargava, Managing Director said, "When we started in August 1981, we knew nothing of car manufacturing. Undaunted, the dedicated team set about selecting the right collaborator. At that point of time, major car producers in the world were not willing to risk an investment in India," remembers Bhargava. What's more, the car selected would have to be small, affordable and fuel efficient. "We were at the final stages of negotiations with a Daihatsu, when we received a proposal from Suzuki. The proposal was not only attractive, they offered us the kind of car we were looking for."

With the millionth car down the assembly line, MUL has irrevocably changed many myths about the Indian automobile industry's capabilities. Even the sceptics grudgingly admit the achievements of MUL, the foremost being that MUL does not smack of inefficiency that public sector undertakings are infamous for. Countering this perception, R.C. Bhargava said, "People on the shop floor are the same throughout the length and breadth of India. It is the managerial staff that makes all the difference. "Just imagine, a large organisation like ours has had no labour or union problems. Workers feel that their managers are not unapproachable. It is this management-worker relationship that has stood MUL in good stead". This has reflected in product quality, making buyers more quality conscious. And it has forced the Indian automobile industry to sit up and take notice. "The ancillary units and OE suppliers had to upgrade to face the stringent quality requirements," said R.C. Bhargava. This has boosted the confidence amongst auto parts manufacturers in scouting for markets in western countries. Many have found new markets beyond the Indian shores.

A HOUSEWIFE'S SKILL BEHIND NAMASTE EXPORTS

Here is another inspiring story of exemplary success achieved by Madhura Bhat. She was only a housewife who even failed to become a lower division clerk, but once she took up making handbags and purses there was no looking back and her business touched Rs. 100 crore turnover, as reported by Allen J. Medonca in the Indian Express. How and why did Madhura Bhat think of taking up work? "It was sheer monotony of daily household chores that led Madhura to rediscover herself." A distinctive feature of her story is her skill in making handbags and purses.

The enterprises took root in a little garage in Bangalore's conservative Basavangudi area with a princely investment of Rs. 5000. For the next two-three years, Madhura's exquisite creations were "bought by friends." When encouraged, Madhura set up a small unit in two rented rooms on Bangalore's J.C. Road and called the enterprises Madhu Crafts. Foreigners, especially Germans working in MICO, the Bangalore-based Bosch company, flocked to the unit. IN 1977, Madhura had her first exhibition. Inquiries from abroad followed and her first batch of accessories, which included leather jackets, were exported to the U.S. Narayana, a practizing lawyer, gradually became involved, accompanying

Madhura abroad a number of times for delicate negotiations. IN 1978, Namaste Exports was launched and the company tied up with Neusa Bekleidungwerke Gmbh for technical and marketing support. When the collaboration ended in 1981, Namaste's turnover had touched Rs. 88 lakhs. The graph kept climbing, thanks to the Bhats' game plan of setting quality, standards and concentrating on backward integration.

Namaste bagged the whole gamut of awards instituted by Council for Leather Exports for being the biggest player in the fact that with earnings per share of Rs. 12, the Company's Rs. 10 scrip commands a premium of Rs. 240 on the bourses. And the fact that Namaste's sales have increased fivefold from Rs. 18 crore in 1988-89 to the projected Rs. 100 crore in 1994. Also, profit has zoomed from Rs. 1.38 crore to Rs. 15 crore.

The international quality of Namaste's garments resulted in haute couture agencies worldwide supplying the latest designs and booking orders from Namaste and then branding them. Namaste made and foreign branded products are now available at Macy's, USA, Harrod's, London, and the boutiques of Macgregor, Lagen Feld, Spengler, Etienner Algier and Daniele Hector on the Continent.

SUITCASE TO A FACTORY

Nalini Sharma looked like your typical woman next door. But within lurks a dynamic business woman whose sari and dress creations, bearing her name, caught the country's imagination. She started from, a suitcase, going around the bazaars of Delhi, picking out unusual saris and selling them to her friends. By the late '70s, Nalini was creating her own designs. She then began to diversify into bed covers, mats, salwar-kameez sets. Ultimately she has achieved total self-sufficiency.

SHOW BUSINESS TO BIG BUSINESS IN FASHION

Ritu Beri, leading fashion designer, highlighting the importance of fashion shows and exhibitions writes that show business is the key to big business. In every country and in every industry there always will be the need for a national show. In addition, which exhibition is considered the main international one will always change, and in fashion it changes faster than in any other field.

The premier collections show began in 1990 as a "women's apparel only event but it has since expanded to cover men's wear, footwear, children's wear, lingerie and swim wear. There are few other product categories the show can expand into, although there is always the potential of such things as store fixtures and information technology. There is aggressive promoting to foreign buyers as seen in the shows held in New York and others such as the jeans wear show in Miami.

BEES MADE GOLDEN MEADOWS

'If life gives you lemons, make lemonade. Life did not really give Sarparveen Kaur lemons. It gave her bees and she had made honey. Six tonnes of it last year. Kaur, 34, has no idea that she'd be living with 50,000 bees in the backyard of her farm near Jalandhar and a vast honey marketing network. Together with her husband, she trains beekeepers, gives them equipment, know-how, even the bees, and then offers to buy their honey and sell it under the Golden Meadows label. Kaur is working on a range of honey-based herbal cosmetics, protein pills made from pollen and a honey by-product that has rejuvenating qualities like ginseng."

A DART OF SUCCESS FOR BLUE DART

About a decade ago, three young men with less than Rs. 30,000 in their pockets and stars in their eyes, embarked on a dream mission to revolutionise the express industry in India. Blue Dart was born. Lack of infrastructure and paucity of funds did not daunt them. Admittedly, it was hectic (not to mention chaotic) at first. Everybody did everything, pick-ups, documentation, connecting shipments onto flights, delivery...But Clyde Cooper, Tushar Jani and Kushroo Dubash persevered on, mindless of all obstacles.

The first taste of success for Blue Dart came when it attained recognition of its potential of business from the Indian exporters. With exports growing at a phenomenal rate, the Indian exporters wanted a door to door service that would ship his samples to buyers around the world within a specified time frame. To this end, Blue Dart tied up with London based Gelco Express International to have access to a global market. Sometime in 1984, Federal Express bought over Gelco Express International. By virtue of this deal Blue Dart was now associated with Federal Express. Blue Dart's alliance with Federal Express opened up a world of opportunities. In turn, Federal Express got a piece of the action in India's burgeoning express industry. The company grew by leaps and bounds, leaving behind a string of milestones.

Today Blue Dart is a multi-crore company. It's operations are controlled from 6 hubs located at Mumbay, Delhi, Chennai, Hyderabad, Bangalore and Erode. The foundation of Blue Dart's success has been the reliability of its service.

MAGIC OF CAN-DO SPIRIT!

"Determination has always been one of my strongest assets. I never let any bowler or situation daunt me. I am equally determined in other areas of life too–if I set my eyes on something I don't rest until I achieve my goal." Sunil Gavaskar.

Achieving success in business is basically not different from succeeding in any other field in life. Luck, chance, coincidence, support or help, which often are associated with success no doubt, at times, do play a very crucial or even decisive role. Yet there is no denying the fact that if we depend solely on these elements and keep waiting, doing nothing, we cannot even think of being successful. Our conscious efforts to achieve success are perhaps more dependable. While concentrating on our own efforts we must be prepared to face future as it unfolds before us. Success can only be achieved through determination and will power.

Coming to the role of making wilful efforts to succeed we must realise first of all the need to have a strong determination–determination of an exemplary nature and shed all fears and apprehensions. Those with weak will power easily give in when difficulties come up. Only those who try and run catch the bus. Others generally miss it. We cannot command success but success often comes to those who dare and act; it soldom goes to the timid who are ever afraid of the consequences, said Jawaharlal Nehru.

LISTEN TO BUSINESS LEADERS!

What is the secret of success of some of the topnotch companies? Their business philosophy or marketing strategies are revealed here.

> **"STRANGE THINGS** happen in life. Sometimes success is born out of failure. So it was with India Today. It was a magazine meant only for Indians living abroad when it started on December 15, 1975. The idea didn't work and only then were copies put out in the Indian market. Added to that, it was launched during the Emergency. It was headed by a chartered accountant turned-printer (that's me) and a staff of half a dozen bright-eyed youngsters whose journalistic experience would fit into a matchbox. Not the most auspicious of beginnings for a national news magazine. And journalists were regarded as such low life that I recall one of the scions of the Modi industrial family asking me, "Aroon, *yaar, tum yeh bhooke aur nange* profession *mein kaise padh gaye ho* (Aroon, how come you've got into this profession of the naked and the hungry)?" Not a comment that lifted my spirits.

But as I said strange things happen in life. Today, INDIA TODAY has a readership of 15.3 million in English and its four regional language editions and is the single most read publication in the country. Its editorial team has grown to 98. The magazine is at the core of a multimedia group with television, Internet, music, books and education divisions. The Group now has a staff strength of 1,009, of which 330 are journalists. And along the way, we fulfilled our original mission by starting, in 1982, an international edition that is very successful and is circulated in 104 countries.

I'm often asked: what's the secret of the success? I don't have a specific answer. I know it is not just one factor but a combination of many. Perhaps it's the fanatical belief that what matters in a publication is editorial excellence and credibility. Spend all your resources in getting it right and the rest of the financial equation will work itself out. For better or worse, we are an editorially driven media organisation as against a marketing one.

Protect your credibility at any cost. You are only as vulnerable as you want to be. If you make a mistake, apologise and try and make amends. Write for the reader, not for journalists. Make your page striking with elegant design, relevant pictures and stylish writing. And above all, never be satisfied."

– Aroon Purie, Editor-in-Chief, *India Today*

"**OUR MARKETNG** strategy is not found on page . . . But, in thinking simple - 'Make our product well, sell it well'. The former, we do with the best of technology, plant and equipment from Italy and Germany. Not to mention, the latest systems-even Robotics. The latter, we achieve with the best of talent. Those who think smart. . . .",

– Liberty Group

Exciting the Customers

"NO DOUBT over the last two decades we have been the leaders in India in fluid power systems. Our products have been an integral part of the ranges offered by industry leaders like Ashok Leyland, BEML, Escorts, HMT, Telco, TAFE and even at ISRO for the Indian Space Programme. But never one to rest on out laurels, we are now on a massive diversification drive. With a new name and a new symbol that signify our entry to even more exciting, state-of-the-art areas. Like advanced hydraulic passenger and cargo lifts. Lifts that can be erected in structures even if they have no provision for lifts. With a technology so advanced that it can give any building 21st century convenience and facilities. This is just the beginning of our steady diversification into more and more exciting and hi-tech products for the Indian customer."

– UT limited.

"NOVEL'S responsible leadership for over a decade has made Netware what it is. The scalable, reliable, robust and feature-rich networking system that's easy to install, use and maintain."

– Netware.

"A LEADER is not born in the board room! Strategic planning, creative thinking, corporate vision. Balmer Lawrie is all set to meet the challenges of the 21st century. Where the management of change has become a way of life. Creating a work culture of looking beyond- even among its youngest managers. A professional blend of human resource development and frontline technology. Effectively absorbing the pressures of growth and diversification. Reaching out to meet the potential of tomorrow."

– Balmer Lawrie & Co. Ltd.

"AT KAJARIA the goal is clear. Leadership worldwide. Leadership in Export. . . . Leadership in Growth...Leadership in Range..Leadership in Technology.

Leadership in Foresight..: At Kajaria the vision is global. We set the trends and opened new markets. This foresight, and good old fashioned hardwork have made us the No. 1 in India. On way to becoming a leader worldwide."

– Kajaria Ceramics Limited.

"WE ARE distinguished as one of the most cost-efficient manufacturers of consumer products. We use the latest manufacturing technology, make optimal use of each resource and, through effective management, achieve a high level of resource productivity."

From the beginning, we have been guided by a set of beliefs, which we committed to writing in 1974. It is up to our customers, employees and shareholders to judge how successful we have been in developing a culture based on these beliefs.

- Respect the individual. People are our greatest asset.
- Achieve and maintain a position of leadership in each of the businesses we are in.
- Pursue all tasks to accomplish them in a superior manner.
- Govern individual and company relationships with the highest standards of conduct and integrity.

- Be close to the customer in action, example and spirit, and ensure superior quality products and services.
- Measure our effectiveness by the long term profits we achieve for our enterprise.
- This, then, is the Wipro Corporation today.

– **Wipro**

"One must possess a strong mind to always improve and to always achieve"

– Mr. Osamu Suzuki, President, **Suzuki Motor Corpn., Japan.**

"**AT PRUDENTIAL**, we believe in making the Right Moves at the Right Time towards more Ambitious Goals. Having concentrated our resources to earn a distinctive position in India, we are constantly striving to exploit new opportunities in the global scenario. With the courage to make tough decisions and the conviction to stand behind them, we face challenges confidently.

The concerted efforts of our dynamic team of professionals has borne unprecedented success for us in a short period. In the interests of jour clients, we have diversified from stock broking into a myriad of financial services. Our range of activities include Merchant Banking, Capital Markets Advisory Services, Investment Broking and Securities Trading, Portfolio Management and allied Financial Services. By following a principle of consistency in quality, our performance has earned the trust of our clients–our most valued asset. Recording a steady progress in results and profitability."

– **Prudential Capital Market Limited**.

"**NO WORDS** are better understood around the world than 'Quality of the highest order. 'Metro Exporters believe that true quality is actually a state of mind rather than a state of product. Because only when our products meet our own thorough quality control standards, are they allowed to be exported worldwide.

In Bicycles & Bicycle components, Engineering products, Textiles & Garments, Dyes & Intermediates, Plastics Drugs & Pharmaceuticals and Chemicals, each of our products has made its mark in UK, Germany, Canada, Japan, Africa, Iran, South America and the far East. And meeting these stringent standards has been extremely easy for Metro Exporters. It's easy when quality is made a state of the mind."

– **Metro Exporters Limited.**

"**THE RANBAXY** Research Foundation has on implicit mission: to provide impetus to research activity and help revive India's scientific tradition. The research awards have been instituted by the Foundation to recognise original, outstanding contributions in the fields of Medical and Pharmaceutical Sciences."

– Ranbaxy.

"**HARD WORK** is not only way to run a young finance company. It's just the only way that succeeds. At India Securities Limited, we can't take things for granted. We don't have offices full of super-specialised divisions, staffed with armies of employees. What we do have is financial savvy, the courage to innovate and a burning desire to succeed. So we customise deals to fit our clients' exact requirements. We cash in on our experience as the Essar Group's financial company. We put in hours of comprehensive and painstaking research and analysis. And then, with all the ground work done, we take the steps that can turn a good transaction into great one. In short, we use every resource we have make sure we meet all our client's needs. Fast. And we never, never take our clients for granted. We can't. If we did, we'd be out of business. In finance, as in nature, only the fittest survive. But as our friend on the left proves, the right attitude more than makes up for any lack of size."

– India Securities Limited.

"**FOR MORE** than 40 years, we have been the leading manufacturer of speciality papers in India. Papers made in a mill with record productivity. With a highly efficient energy-saving system. And environment-friendly raw materials. Yet our people remained far from satisfied.

Because within their hearts they knew that they could still show industry the way to superior product quality, resource utilisation and cost efficiency. A fact that we too had acknowledged as vital for success in the international market.

We discovered that our people already had glowing embers within them. Our discussing the issues at stake with the Unions and the workmen, our explaining of objectives only helped set them fully ablaze. To a man, the complete workforce wanted to show the world that they and their products could come up to international standards.

They realised that the surest way to better their lot was to better the company's performance. Of course, this would mean new technologies and increased capacity (from 13,500 tonnes per annum to 33,000). But the proposed training and redeployment programmers would not just take care of it–they would help exceed the norms. Something only to expected from the culture of productivity.

Thus was signed a long-term agreement on 1st November, 1993, marking the beginning of a completely new era for our people.

And for the people of West Bengal.

How did we achieve this?

I.T.C. Limited's decision to first invest Rs. 20 crores in 1989 (soon after its takeover) and now Rs. 80 crores, helped. After all, no one had done so in an existing unit in West Bengal in recent times. The State Government's attitude helped. Without speedy clearances and full support, we may not have accomplished so much, so soon.

The vastly improved infrastructure in the region helped. Take power, transport, raw materials–we couldn't be better off anywhere else in the country.

Above all, our people helped. Because they really are our powerhouse. Our most valuable source of energy.

So the next time you come across at Tribeni Tissues' paper, think about the one thing that made it possible. People.'

– I.T.C. Limited Tribeni Tissues Division.
– "*The vision to lead, the will to succeed.*"

THE STORY began in 1943. Those were the fading years of the British Raj. The post Quit India scenario was sweeping the Indian masses. And the Swadeshi movement was at its zenith. That's when the textile industry saw the dawn of a new era emerging. Balwant Textiles came into being. The objective–to produce top quality cotton yarn. To be able to supply the basic raw material for the fabric of all Indians-cotton. Since then, the company has only grown stronger in its objective to give of its best. Only the best quality cotton from some of the most fertile belts of India is accepted. Nothing less will do. This penchant for quality continues to be one of Balwant's greatest strengths.

Every single process of manufacturing right from procurement of raw material to the finished cotton yarn is monitored by experts. No stone is left unturned to ensure the best results.

And the results speak for themselves. Today, Balwant Textiles enjoys a prestigious list of clients. Sales turnover has shown a healthy growth, more so, over the past three years. Above all, Balwant Textiles commands the trust and confidence of the textile industry. Qualities that from the basis of a strong and lasting relationship. One that can stand the test of time. Andus on to even greater strength.

– **Balwant Textiles Mills Limited** [Widely known as Marathe Textile Mills, Miraj (Maharashtra)].

THE SHREE Krishna Group started in 1958 with a single small unit to manufacture speciality fabrics. Today, it is the biggest manufacturer of such fabrics in the whole of Asia.

– **The Shree Krishna Group of Companies, Mumbay**.

AT TATA Steel, the pace of change is decided not by top management alone but through the Total Team concept-creative solutions shared from the bottom to the top.

Today, responsible decision making by workers is the new way of solving problems at Tata Steel. Networking across levels is creating an environment of innovation, confidence and pride on the shop-floor, in every plant.

And the results? When the state-of-the-art 'G' Blast Furnace was commissioned, it broke all records by producing to capacity within 25 days–a world record. A true tribute to team work at Tata Steel, because today, every Tata Steel worker can say with pride, "This plant is mine".

And that is the pride and confidence that reflects the spirit of the New India.

– **Reflected by the Tata Team and Tata Technology at Tata Steel**

Technological Leadership

At the Anand Group we started out with the attitude of leadership. And, a vision that stressed that if we were to be the leaders, we had to ensure growth ahead of the market.

It is this philosophy that has been virtually every company in the Anand fold on the top. Our brands are among the leaders in engine bearings, piston rings and gaskets. When it comes to shock absorbers, struts and filters, they are number one in their respective fields.

With nineteen international collaborations and associations, fifteen companies, and 2300 motivated people, we now look forward to consolidating our existing strengths. Just so that we are ready for the 21st century, for greater global participation and a turnover that exceeds Rs. 1000 crores.

Give a man orders and he'll do the task reasonably well. But let him set his own targets. Give him freedom and authority and the task become a personal mission.

We have been able to build teams of dedicated people with this "I Can" spirit.

Our plant in North India is expected to commission early next year.

– Anand Group.

SOMETIMES, A name can say a lot. Abut business ethics and value system, hallowed traditions, good breeding and a model to live up to.

Among corporate names, MAFATLAL stands with the best and the most respected. And Mafatlal Finance has, if we do say so ourselves, lived up to the name it has inherited.

– Mafatlal

TECLO. A company that has withstood competition from the world's most reputed auto-makers, staying ahead with a combination of innovation, marketing savvy and sheer product superiority. Today it remains the country's leading automobile company.

The Tata group is proud of having Telco as one of its members. The company embodies the values and beliefs of the group. Innovation, integrity and dynamism. Strengths that each and every one of the group's 270,000 employees considers his personal responsibility. Strengths that have given the Tata group an unassailable reputation for quality.

Behind the group's turnover of Rs. 15,000 crores and wide range of products and services stands a century of trust and a tradition of firsts. Backing every product and service that bears the mark you see on this page. The mark of Tata.

– Tata India's Most Trusted Mark.

WHAT WE have achieved so far has been done with Indian skills, with Indian technologies, in the Indian environment. We have demonstrated to ourselves that we have the ability to take charge of again next year, the fact of Torrent will have changed. The projects that we had taken up earlier are now nearing fruition.

Close to the customer: There are far too many Indian companies that have to learn that running a business is not about buying, converting and selling, but is about satisfying customer needs..

At Torrent, our earliest successes came from learning this lesson. We built dominant positions in niche markets by making combination products, in a market where other manufacturers were asking patients to buy two products separately and consume them together.

By staying close to the customer, we built a dominant position in psychotropic drugs and in cardiovascular drugs. We are now developing a strong position in anti-infective and in infusions.

The protected business environment, in particular the regulated capacity regime, that Indian companies have operated in over the last four decades, has resulted in the consumer being forgotten. When we talk about competing today, we mean competing for customer patronage and loyalty, not competing for licenses. Businesses that do not understand this change cannot flourish in a free market.

Staying for the long haul: All these issues–thinking globally, getting close to the customer, establishing high quality standards in every area of the business, investing in building the business-imply a long-term commitment to developing a globally competitive business. There is little point in attempting to build such a business unless one intends to see the process through.

– Torrent Pharmaceuticals Ltd.

"I FEEL sorry that we have not taken full advantage of the possibilities in our country–looking at the availability of raw materials, our talent, our entrepreneurship and managerial abilities which so many other developing countries are lacking."

– Ramakrishna Bajaj.

7

Helping Hands to Your Success

Hereunder are given brief details/some important addresses of governmental and non-governmental agencies that could be useful to you in setting up your own business. These agencies provide a number of services ranging from entrepreneurial training, technical consultancy, financial assistance etc. for those interested in self-employment.

SMALL INDUSTRIES SERVICE INSTITUTES (SISIs)

There are 28 SISIs and 30 branch SISIs set up in State capitals and other industrial cities all over the country. Their functions include:

- Interface between Central and State Governments
- Technical support services
- Entrepreneur Development Programmes
- Developmental efforts for SSI
- Promotional programmes for SSI

SSIs and its Branches have common facility workshops in various trades. There are at present 45 such common facility workshops attached to SISIs/Branch SISIs.

FACILITIES OFFERED TO SSIs

Regional Testing Centres (RTCs)

Testing facilities are being extended through 4 Regional Testing Centres at Kolkata, Mumbai, Chennai and New Delhi and Field Testing Stations for raw materials, semi finished products and the end products primarily manufactured in the small scale sector. These centres have been equipped with the basic testing facilities in the disciplines of chemical, mechanical, electrical, metallurgy and metrology. These Testing Centres besides rendering facilities, assist in quality upgradation aspects and provide training in testing and quality control besides consultancy in testing and quality management and in process quality control systems.

Tool Rooms/Tool Design Institutes

Ten Tool Rooms are in existence to cater to the tooling needs of small scale industries. The existing ones are located at: Kolkata, Ludhiana, Jalandhar, Hyderabad, Nagpur, Bhubaneshwar, Indore, Jamshedpur, Ahemdabad and Aurangabad. State Government-run-Tool Rooms are at Lucknow, Delhi, Bangalore, Mysore and Goa.

Tool Rooms provide the following services

- Assistance in tool design
- Manufacture of tools, jigs, fixtures, moulds & dies etc.
- Training facilities to tool makers.
- Common service facilities
- Consultancy.

Product-cum-Process Development Centres

Four Centres are in existence and two new Centres are at Firozabad (UP) for Glass Industry and Kannauj (UP) for Flavour and Fragrance. They are designed to work basically as R&D Institutions to carry out advanced developmental work in the concerned fields. Existing centres are at Meerut, Agra, Ramnagar and Mumbai. Two State Government-run-PPDCs are at Ludhiana and one at Ambala. Two more are being set up at Batala and Ludhiana. Their functions include:

- To serve as research and development institutions in areas in dense industry cluster.
- Product design and innovation
- Product and process improvement and development of improved packaging techniques.
- Common facility centre.
- Manpower development/training.

Central Footwear Training Institutes

CFTIs are in Agra and Chennai. CFTC Kolkata is functioning and CFTC Mumbai is under implementation. Their functions include:

- Training of manpower for footwear industry.
- Developing designs/new types of footwear to promote exports.

Associate Institutions–Training

There are three specialised institutions to undertake efforts in training and human resource development. They carry out entrepreneurship development programmes and meet the specialised training needs of the industry. The Institutions are:

- Integrated Training Centre (Inds.), Nilokheri, Haryana.
- National Institute for Small Industry Extension and Training (NISIET), Hyderabad.
- National Institute for Entrepreneurship and Small Business Development (NIESBUD), New Delhi.
- Indian Institute of Entrepreneurship, Guwahati.

List of Small Industries Service Institutes & Branch SISIs is given in Chapter 9.

SIDO Services

Small Industries Development Organisation provides a comprehensive range of industrial extension services ranging from product identification to product marketing as given below:

Modernisation/In-Plant Studies

These services are available through the RTCs, Field Testing Stations and the Workshops attached to the SISIs.

Sub-Contract Exchanges

Fifteen Sub-contract Exchanges have been established in major SISIs to promote interaction between small and large units. They organise vendor development programmes and promote ancillarisation.

Escort Services

SISIs and its associated institutions promote small scale industries through escort services by providing consultancy, information services, technical services and other services with following one.

- Economic information
- Project Identification and formulation
- Feasibility studies

- Industrial designing
- Product development
- Marketing advice and assistance, and
- Export Promotion

Entrepreneurship Development and Training

They include various types of EDP programmes run by SISIs, Branch SISIs and Associate Institutions. Technical training is provided to beginners/workers and a host of management inputs are given to entrepreneurs/investors. Training in technical skill development is given to technicians and workers in various workshops, Testing Centres and Tool Rooms.

Integrated Infrastructure Development Scheme

The scheme is envisaged to augment the infrastructural development facilities in rural and backward areas to promote industrial development.

Salient Features

- Cost of each project is around Rs. 5 crores including cost of land, Equity by Government of India upto Rs. 2 crores and balance by loan through SIDBI.
- Project size of each centre would be around 15 to 20 hectares.
- Scheme will create and augment infrastructural needs within the project are a with full technological back up.

Export Promotion

Trade exhibitions are held abroad and export worthy SSI units are given opportunity and assistance in exhibiting their selected items in these exhibitions. Imports under some of the schemes are allowed without payment of customs duty or at concessional rates of customs duty.

(**Note:** Export promotion is done through a number of other schemes, which can be ascertained from the SIDO offices.)

Central Government Incentives/Facilities Concessions

Central Government provides a host of incentives and facilities to small enterprises.

Fiscal Incentives

Excise duty exemptions and concessions are available to small scaleu nits with turnover under the excise duty exemption scheme. These exemptions and concessions are available to both registered and unregistered SSI Units.

Reservation of Items Manufactured/Reserved for Production and Purchase

Under this scheme certain items have been reserved exclusively for manufacture in SSI sector, for purchase from SSI sector.

HOW TO ARRANGE FINANCE?

A network of State Financial Corporations, National Small Industries Corporation, State Small Industries Corporations, Commercial Banks, Cooperative Banks, Regional Rural Banks provide financial assistance to small scale units. Small Industries Development Bank of India provides refinance to the industrial loans advanced by these institutions to small scale sector.

State Financial Corporations (SFCs)

State Financial Corporations grant term loan for the purchase of land, construction of factory premises and purchase of machinery and equipment for the setting up of new industries or for expansion or modernisation of the existing ones. SFCs generally prescribe a margin of 25% and allow an initial holiday of two years for the loan repayment (this period can be increased to five years in backward districts).

National Small Industries Corporation (NSIC) and State Small Industries Corporations (SSICs)

NSIC and SSICs supply machinery on hire-purchase basis to small scale and ancillary industries.

Single point registration scheme of NSIC was introduced in 1976 to avoid the need for multiplicity of registration by the SSI units with different purchasing agencies like DGS & D, Railways, Defence etc. The NSIC enlists the SSI units to undertake supply of various items needed by the Government Departments/Public Sector Undertakings.

The National Small Industries Corporation Ltd. (A Government of India Enterprise) NSIC Bhavan, Okhla Industrial Estate, New Delhi 110020 offers a wide range of services and facilities to the small scale sector. Some of its important schemes are as under:

(a) Marketing Assistance Scheme

(b) Equipment Leasing Scheme

(c) Government Stores Purchase Programme

(d) Turnkey offers for Small Industrial Projects

(e) Hire Purchase for Promotion of SSI

(f) Prototype Development and Training Centres

(g) Financial services for Small Enterprises

Commercial Banks

Commercial Banks provide short term and medium term financial assistance to small scale units. Short term credit facilities are granted for working capital requirements like those for raw materials, goods-in-process, finished products, bills receivables and book debts. Medium term loans are granted for the acquisition of land, construction of factory premises, purchase of machinery and equipment and operative expenses. These loans are generally granted for periods ranging from five to seven years.

Small Industries Development Bank of India (SIDBI)

Small Industries Development Bank of India–the apex bank for small scale industries extends assistance of SSI units through various schemes. All projects in the small scale sector are normally eligible for assistance.

State Govts./UT Govts. Incentives/Facilities/Concessions

In order to avail these facilities SSI units are required to be registered with the Directorate of Industries of State/UT Governments. Some of the important facilities/incentives provided are:–

- Land, developed plots and sheds in industrial estates on easy terms.
- Necessary infrastructure at developed sites e.g. power, water, communication.
- Capital subsidy on investment on fixed assets in selected backward areas at varying rates.
- Sales tax deferment/tax holiday.
- Relief on octroi, electricity duty, stamp duty.
- Interest subsidy.
- Power subsidy, subsidy on generating sets.
- Financial assistance for preparation of project reports.
- Seed capital for starting projects.
- Subsidy for obtaining technical know-how.
- Subsidy for testing the products in approved test houses.

All these concessions are not uniform in the States. Their content, nature and quantum of assistance also varies from state to state and UTs.

State Small Industries Corporations assist in procurement of raw materials, marketing etc. District Industries Centres play a crucial role in the promotion and development of small industries.

Export Credit Guarantee Corporation of India (ECGC)

Regd. Office: Express Towers, 10th floor, Nariman Point Mumbay 400021. *Northern Regional Office:* Antriksh Bhawan, 8th Floor, 22, Kasturba Gandhi Marg, New Delhi 110001. Tele: 23317505, 23319525, 23320853 Telex: 031-6538, CABLE-ERICBAID Fax: (011) 23317708.

ECGC is a company wholly owned by the Government of India. It functions under the administrative control of the Ministry of Commerce and is managed by a Board of Directors representing Government, Banking, Insurance, Trade, Industry, etc. It offers a wide range of policies to cover practically every type of export transaction.

Covers Issued by ECGC

The covers issued by ECGC can be divided broadly into four groups:

(i) Standards policy issued to exporters to protect them against payment risks involved in exports on short-term credit and Small Exporter's Policy issued for the same purpose to exporters with small export;

(ii) Specific Policies designed to protect Indian firms against payment risks involved in (a) exports on deferred terms of payment (b) services rendered to foreign parties and (c) construction works and turnkey projects undertaken abroad;

(iii) Financial guarantees issued to banks in India to protect them from risks of loss involved in their extending financial support to exporters at the pre shipments as well as postshipment stages; and

(iv) Special schemes, viz., Transfer Guarantee meant to protect banks which add confirmation to letters of Credit opened by foreign banks. Insurance cover for Buyer's Credit, Line of Credit, Overseas Investment Insurance and Exchange Fluctuation Risk Insurance.

Additional Useful Information:

Apart from the above organisations helping the entrepreneurs, we have also included addresses of some other specialised agencies/other information which may prove useful to the prospective entrepreneurs. These are given in the following annexures:

Annexure VI

- Specialised Agencies
- Important Technical Consultancy Organisations
- Addresses useful for prefeasibility studies
- Institute of Entrepreneurship Development (IEDs) and Centres for Entrepreneurship Development (CEDs)
- Export Promotion Councils
- Government Organisations for Export-Import Trade

Annexure VII

- Mini-Micro Enterprise Ideas:
  - Engineering & Allied Industry
  - Chemical & Cosmetic Industries
  - Textile Industries
  - Paper & Stationery Industry
  - Agro based Plastic Industry.

Annexure VIII

- Low Technology, Low Investment Business Ideas:
  - Mineral based Industries
  - Agro Based Industries
  - Engineering and Non-conventional Energy
  - Textile (excluding Khadi)
  - Electronic Industry

Annexure IX

Service Sector Opportunities.

8

Some Courses for Self-Employment

Indian Institute of Technology, Centre for Consultancy and Sponsored Research, Chennai offers M.S. (Entrepreneurship) a Master's level programme, for Engineering are Technology graduates, leading to **M.S. in Entrepreneurship.** The objective of this programme is to expose the young engineers to the field of entrepreneurship development and to provide them with excellent facilities for hi-tech product development. It is tailor made for those who have an urge to start their own industries. **Eligibility:** Degree in any of the disciplines of engineering technology or appearing for the same are eligible to apply. A minimum GATE score of 70 percentile is essential for admission. **Fellowship:** Candidates admitted to the M.S. Programme are eligible for fellowship, as per the Government of India norms. **Last date:** April.

Indian Institute of Entrepreneurship & Management, IIEM, 13, Institutional Area, Lodi Road, New Delhi 110003 offers (a) Integrated Advance Courses in **Management/Entrepreneurship,** (b) One year Specialisation Courses in Management/Entrepreneurship, (c) One year Professional Courses, (d) One to Six months for Short Course (Evening). **Eligibility:** (i) *Integrated Advance Courses/Specialisation:* Graduation or 3 years Diploma, or also 10+2 on clearning one year Foundation Course. (ii) *Entrepreneurship Development for Women:* Graduation. (iv) *All Professional Courses*: 10+2. **Notification:** July. **Last date:** August.

Centre for Electronics Design and Technology (An autonomous institute under Department of Electronics, Government of India) Sas Nagar: (Mohali) near Chandigarh, offers six-week **Entrepreneurship Development Programme** (How to set up an Entrepreneurial Venture in

Electronics and Computers) sponsored jointly by Department of Science and Technology, Govt. of India, IDBI, IFCI and ICICI.

The Centre caters to the training, consultancy, design and product development needs of electronics industry and allied sectors and also promotes potential entrepreneurship, various loan schemes; case studies, standardisation, trade and patent laws, materials management, marketing management personnel management and labour laws, book keeping, fund flow, testing specification, technical considerations, ancillary, development, import export and computers applications, video sessions, market survey, industrial visits and achievement motivation training for setting up an industrial unit.

The programme also includes guidance on preparation of Project Profile.

Eligibility: Degree in any branch of Science or Diploma/Degree in any branch of Engineering/Technology or persons having relevant background.

Further details may be had from the Director, CEDT, A-34, Phase VIII, Industrial Area, SAS Nagar, Mohali, (Punjab) 160059.

Haryana Delhi Industrial Consultants Ltd. (Hardicon)—A joint venture of IFCI, IDBI, ICCI, Banks and SFC's offers **Entrepreneurship Development Programme** (EDP) for Women under the sponsorship of Small Industries Development Bank of India (IDBI). The Programme trains, assistance and guidance in selection of the product, market survey to enable trainees to start and run their unit successfully. You are provided escort services and assistance in getting your loan and seed capital under Mahila Udhyam Nidhi Scheme (MUN) of SIDBI.

Eligibility: Women with working knowledge of Hindi/English are eligible.

Course Fee: SIDBI is contributing substantially to the course fee. Participants are required to pay prescribed charges as course fee/ preparation of project report. Further details can be had from the Course Co-ordinator (EDP), Haryana-Delhi Industrial Consultants Ltd., D-28, Flatted Factory Complex, Jhandewalan, New Delhi 110055 (Telephone 27538814, 27536224).

Small Industries Service Institute, Deptt. of Small Scale, Agro & Rural Industries, Govt of India, Ministry of Industry, Industrial Area=B, Opp. Sangeet Cinema, Ludhiana 141003, offers **Entrepreneurship Motivational Programme** for unemployed.

FICCI Ladies' Organisation, Federation House, Tansen Marg, New Delhi 110001 (Ph 23319251 to 23319261) arranges **Entrepreneurship Development Programmes** for training, Support and guidance to women for starting their own small industry, from time to time. Further details can be had from the above address.

Small Industries Service Institute, Okhla Industrial Estate, New Delhi 110020, offers part-time specialised course in **Materials Management** for the residents of the Union Territory of Delhi, Distt. Faridabad of Haryana & Distt. Ghaziabad & Noida of U.P.

Objective: The main emphasis of the programmes is to raise the motivational level of the participants and promote their capacity to manage their enterprises scientifically. **Duration:** Three weeks. **Eligibility:** Small Scale Industrialists, their senior employees and prospective entrepreneur.

Prescribed application form and further details may be had from the Director, Small Industries Service Instt., Okhla Indl. Estate, New Delhi 110020, or Asst. Director I/C, Balsahyog E.C., Opp. Nirula Hotel, Connaught Place, New Delhi.

Small Industries Service Institute, Ministry of Industry, Govt. of India, Okhla Indl. Estate, New Delhi 110020, offers **Reduce Cost-Increase Productivity Specialised Course** in Cost Reduction. **Who can apply:** Small scale industrialists and their employees and prospective entrepreneurs located in the Union Territory of Delhi, districts of Ghaziabad & Faridabad.

Further details may be had from the Director, Small Industries Service Instt., Okhla Indl. Estate, New Delhi 110020, or the Asstt. Director I/C, Balsahyog, Extension Centre, Opp. Nirula Hotel, Connaught Place, New Delhi.

Burhani Institute of Business Entrepreneurship (B.I.B.E.) offers an opportunity to become achievement-oriented Business Entrepreneurs/ Industrialists through its three-year full-time intensive training programme leading to the Institute's **Diploma in Business Entrepreneurship**.

Eligibility: Holders of Higher Secondary level (HSC/ISC/CBSE) qualification of any recognised Board of Examinations or Bachelor's Degree in any discipline. Application forms can be had from Burhani Institute of Business Entrepreneurship, Plot No. 31, Burhani Manzil, Saifee Park, Church Road, Marol, Andheri (E), Mumbay 400059 (Ph 28371346).

Training Programme on How to Start an Export Business covering India's Foreign Trade, Trade Policy and Procedures, Export Marketing, Export Licensing, Customs, Banking, etc., is offered by FICCI Ladies Organisation Federation House, Tansen Marg, New Delhi 110001.

Small Industries Service Institute, Department of Small Scale, Agro & Rural Industries, Industrial Area "B", Ludhiana 141003 offer one-month **Entrepreneurship Development Programme on Leather Products** conducted at Govt. Quality Marking Centre, Ind. Area, Jalandhar (Seats 30). **Eligibility: Minimum** Matric pass. **Age:** 18 year & above, resident of Punjab or UT Chandigarh. Selection is made on the basis of an interview at SISI, Ludhiana. For further details you may contact the Administrative officer. **Notification:** published in the prominent national dailies and Employment News during, the month of September.

Small Industries Service Institute, Narsapur Cross Roads, Balanagar, Hyderabad 500037 offers the following **Skill Based Entrepreneurship Development Programme** at Hyderabad to educated unemployed youth: 1. Motor rewinding & Transformer winding (10 weeks,), 2. Screen Printing (4 weeks).

Eligibility: Age 18-35 years as on the date of commencement of training. Qualification: 10th Passed. Preference is given to experience candidates in their respective fields. **Objective:** To Motivate & Guide Educated unemployed youth in setting up their own Small Scale Industrial Units. For further details you may contact the Director, SISI, Balanagar, Hyderabad 37.

Government of India, Ministry of Industry, Small Industries Service Institute, Okhla Industrial Estate, New Delhi-110002, offers who weeks Training Programme **on Ready-made Garments for Women Entrepreneurs.** The training covers related aspects of starting a small scale industry and also provides practical training on designing & working on industrial machines for garments manufacturing.

Eligibility: 10+2 passed. **Age:** 18 to 35 years. For further details contact Hosiery Section of Small Industries Service Institute Okhla, New Delhi 110020.

Date of Advertisement: August.

National Economic Planning Techniques offers two-year full-time residential programme in **Planning and Entrepreneurship. Eligibility:** Applicants should have completed 10+1 school system with 2/3/4 years' education in colleges/institutes in any discipline. Candidates with Mathematics at Higher Secondary level are preferred. An entrance test is conducted for admission. Further details can be had from the National Economic Planning Techniques, Institutional Area, Lodi Road, New Delhi 110003.

Central Institute of Fisheries Education, Mumbay, offers

(1) Management of Fresh Water Fish Seed Farm

(2) Management of Brackish water Fish Farm

(3) Management of Giant Freshwater Prawn Hatchery.

Eligibility: Farmers and entrepreneurs preferably graduates in Science of not less than 40 years age. Candidates desirous to seek admissions to the above courses may get in touch with the Scientist in charge (Ext Division), Central Institute of Fisheries Education (ICAR) Deemed University, Andheri (W) Versova, Mumbay 400061.

Directorate General of Employment and Training, (Govt of India, Ministry of Labour), Sector 1, Noida 201301 offers to women candidates admission to the course of **Business Services** conducted at NVTI Noida.

The course is divided in two modules: 1. **Enterprises management 2. Enterprise launching and resourcing.**

Further details and application procedure can be had from the office of the Principal, NVTI, Sector 1, Noida.

Hartron, Young Entrepreneurs Support Division, ERDC, 1 Udyog Vihar, Gurgaon 122016 offers the following facilities to entrepreneurs with ideas to set up manufacturing units for Electronic products without investing in capital equipment.

If you are an entrepreneur with a product idea or design and have the confidence to market the product, then HARTRON can help you launch you product without going in for land, building or equipment with your working capital. You can get the product designed, assembled, tested and packed at our facility at Udyog Vihar, Gurgaon, and market in with your efforts. No long term contract is envisaged and you can change your product as often as you want. There is no restriction, upper or lower, on volume of production. You can get a few pieces made or as large a number as you like.

it provides all assembly facilities including wave soldering with component insertion on SS/PTH PCBS design and test facilities and expert advice on all technical matters.

Small Industries Service Institute, Government of India, Ministry of Industry, Guindy, Chennai 600032, offers six months' Advance Training Programme in **Gem Cutting and Polishing** Course. **Highlights:** The programme covers full of practical on gem cutting and polishing (mainly American diamond) procuring of raw materiais, marketing, export possibilities and marketing assistance.

Centre for the Development of Glass Industry, (UNIDO/UNDP Assisted Project), A Govt. of India Registered Society, S.N. Marg, Firozabad (UP) 283203 (Ph 2821672, 2823886) Centre for the Development of Glass Industry has been established at Firozabad, with joint assistance of UNIDO/UNDP, Govt. of UP and Govt. of India products and develop new glass melting and forming technologies ensuring proper utilisation of raw materials energy resources and assimilation of relevant energy recovery systems by the glass industry and protection of environment. The Centre is imparts training course in the following fields:

1. Chemical Lab Practices (2½-month), 2. **Technique in Glass Cutting** (6-month), 3. **Advance course in Glass Toys Manufacturing** (4-month). **Eligibility:** (a) Lab. Practices B.Sc. (with Chemistry as one of the subjects) b) Glass Cutting & Glass Toys: School Leaving Certificate. **Age:** Above 18 year. **Preference:** (1) Local entrepreneurs (2) SC/ST/OBC (3) Female (4) Factory Sponsored. Further details can be had from the Principal Director, CDGI, S.N. Marg, Farozabad 283203.

Central Institute of Plastics Engineering & Technology (A Government of India Society) Guindy, Chennai 600032 CIPET offers the following long-term training programmes at Headquarters Channai and its Extension Centres at Ahmedabad, Amritsar, Bhubaneswar, Bhopal, Hyderabad, Lucknow and Imphal.

(1) 1 year **Post Graduate Diploma in Plastics Engineering**. **Eligibility:** A Degree in Mech/Chem/Production/Polymer Engg. **Age Limit:** 26 years.

(2) 1 year **P.G. Diploma in Plastics Processing Tech**. **Eligibility: A:** Degree in Science with Chemistry/Physics Major. **Age:** 24 years.

(3) 1 year **Post Graduate Diploma in Plastics Testing and Conversion Tech**. **Eligibility:** A Degree in science with Chemistry/Physics Major. Age Limit: 24 years.

(4) 1 year **Post Diploma in Plastics Mould Design**. **Eligibility:** Diploma in Mech/Plastics Tech/Tool Engg/Plastics Engg/ Equivalent. **Age:** 24 years.

(5) 3-year **Diploma in Plastics Mould Technology**. **Eligibility:** A Pass in SSC/10th Std. with Maths, English & Science. **Age:** 18 years.

(6) 2-year **Diploma in Plastics Mould Making Technicians**. **Eligibility:** ITI in Turning/Fitting/Machinist. **Age:** 22 years.

Courses offered at Channai (HQ) 1 to 6, Ahmedabad Centre 1 to 6, Amritsar Centre 2 & 5, Bhubaneswar Centre 2 & 4, Bhopal Centre 2, 4 & 5, Hyderabad Centre 2 & 4, Imphal Centre 2, Lucknow Centre 2 & 4.

Admission Regulations and General Instructions

Selection is based on academic record, a pass in the Joint Entrance Examination and Personal Interview which is conducted during July at Ahmedabad, Agartala, Amritsar, Aizwal, Bangalore, Bhopal, Bhubaneswar, Mumbay, Kolkata, Chandigarh, Cochin, Delhi, Dimapur, Gorakhpur, Guwahati, Hyderabad, Imphal, Jabalpur, Jaipur, Lucknow, Channai, Patna, Pune, Rajkot, Shimla, Tiruchirapalli and Visakhapatnam.

Limited Hostel accommodation is available at all the centres and is allocated on a First-come first served basis.

Further details can be had from Senior Manager (Trg. & Plg.) Corporate CIPET, Guindy, Channai 600032. Application forms can also be obtained from the Extension Centres located at Channai, Amritsar, Bhubaneswar, Bhopal, Hyderabad, Lucknow and Imphal.

National Council for Cement and Building Materials, Centre for Human Resource and Continuing Education, M-10, South Extension Part-II, Ring Road, New Delhi 110049 (Ph 26440133, Fax 91-11-2 6468868) offers the following Training Programmes:

(i) **Long Term Course** (1) 1-year PG Diploma Course in Cement Technology (LTC).

(ii) **Short Term Courses:** A. Cement Technology (1) 5-days Raw mix design, quality control, process & operation and maintenance of VSK mini cement plant (2) 5-days Advanced course in mine planning and quarrying practices (3) 5-days Total productive maintenance in cement plants - systems approach (4) 5-days Testing and calibration of Instrument/equipment in a cement plant (5) 5-days Environmental audit and pollution control in cement industry (6) 5-days Cement Rotary Kiln automation and optimisation (7) 5-days Advanced course in size reduction in cement manufacture B (8) 5-days Selection, testing and evaluation of concrete making materials (9) 2-weeks Concrete Technology (10) 5-days Concrete mix design and quality control (11) 5-days Advances in concrete construction practices (12) 5-days Repairs and rehabilitation of concrete structures (13) 5-days Use of flyash and other newer materials in concrete construction (14) 5-days Quality assurance in concrete construction.

(iii) **Simulator Based Courses** (1) 6-days Operation of large precalciner kilns (2) 6-days Operation of roller mills and ball mills (3) 5-days Computerised control in kiln operation (4) 5-days Operation of preheaterkilns (5) 6-days Operation of large precalcine kilns (6) 5-days Computerised control in kiln operation (8) 6-days Operation of roller mills and ball mills.

(iv) **Workers' Development Programmes** (1) 5-days Maintenance of heavy earth moving equipment and machinery.

(v) **Contact Training Programmes:** Trailor-made contact programmes to meet the specific requirements of individuals/ sponsored organisations in various areas are organised on mutually convenient dates at NCB Units for a period of 2 to 5 days. Areas covered are: Colorimetric methods of analysis for cement and raw materials; EDTA methods of analysis for cement and raul moterials; Estimation of free silica; Estimation of chloride in cement; Estimation of alkalies in cement by flame photometer; Testing of pozzolanic maters; Proximate and ultimate analysis of coal; Evaluation and quality assessment of limestone and cement clinker through optical microscopy; Testing and calibration of laboratory equipment in a cement plant; Physical testing of cement; AAS methods of analysis for cement and raw materials; Mineralogical analysis of clinker/cement/raw materials by XRD; Analysis of hardened concrete, etc.

(vi) **Special Group Training Programmes** (a) Programmes to be organised on request from India and overseas Cement/ Construction Industry and agencies like UNIDO, etc. (b) Programmes of short duration to be organised in the areas such as Operation and maintenance of ESPs, kilns and mills, Conditions monitoring of equipment and machinery, Energy conservation and audit, Cement quality and consumer requirements, Quality System documentation, Auditing to ISO 9000/IS 14000, Management, etc. in different cities/cement plants wherever sizeable interest exists. (c) Programmes to be organised on cement manufacturing technology of 8 weeks duration. For further details please Fax or write to the Director General NCCBM.

It also offers 1-year **Post Graduate Diploma Course in Cement Technology**. The course have two streams - One for engineering graduates who are specialising in process technology including operation and maintenance and other for M.Sc., B.Sc. who are specialising in testing and quality control in cement manufacture.

Eligibility: Graduates in Science (with a minimum of 55% marks and with Physics, Chemistry and Mathematics and also Engineering graduates in mechanical, chemical, ceramics, electrical, electronics or instrumentation disciplines are eligible to apply.

Duration: One year. **Venue:** NcB-Ballabgarh (Haryana). **Course Fee Participants:** Rs. 70,000/- for sponsored participants.

Admission

(1) Preference is given to candidates sponsored by industry/ Government departments/undertakings, etc.

(2) For non-sponsored candidates, selection is through a written test and/or interview.

(3) Minimum qualifying marks may be relaxed in the case of sponsored candidates.

Further details can be had from the Director General, National Council for Cement and Building Materials, M-10, South Extension-II, New Delhi 110049 (Fax 91-11-26468868).

Central Footwear Training Centre, SISI, 65/1, G.S.T. Road, Chennai 600032 offers 2-year **Advanced Course in Footwear Technology Eligibility**: **Age:** 18-25 year as on November 1. **Qualification:** 10+2 passed or equivalent from any recognised Higher Secondary School. **Desirable:** Graduate in any discipline or diploma/degree in Engineering/ Technology. One-year practical experience sponsored by registered S.S.I. Footwear Unit. Application form & prospectus can be had from the Deputy Director I/C, CFTC, Channai on written request together with demand draft for requisite charges in favour of Deputy Director. **Notification:** September. **Last date:** October. For further details you may contact the Deputy Director I/C, CFTC, Channai (Ph 22341529).

Central Leather Research Institute, (Council of Scientific & Industrial Research), Adyar, Channai 600020 offers the following **Modular Training Programmes** on Cutting and Clicking, Assembling and Stitching, Lasting and Finishing, and Pattern Making suited for service as Master Technicians, Supervisory Personnel and Trainers:

(a) Certificate courses in Footwear/Leather Goods/Leather Garments (26-week duration); and

(b) Diploma courses in Leather Goods/Leather Garments (40-week duration).

Eligibility: Age: Maximum 30 years as on 1st July, relaxable in deserving cases. **Qualification:** For course (a) 5-0% in 10+2 or equivalent.

For (b) 50% in SSLC or equivalent. Selection is made through an entrance test, interview and case of candidates with experience in Leather Industry, a trade test. Application form & prospectus can be had from the Head, Education & Training Division, CLRI, Adyar, Channai on payment of requisite charges. **Notification:** February. **Last date:** March 15. Entrance test & interview in April.

Small Industries Service Institute (Government of India, Ministry of Industry), Kanjany Road, Ayyanthole, Thrissur 680003 (Kerala) offers **Training Facilities for Artisans and workers of Small Scale Industries:**

1. **Manufacture of Foot-wear & Leather Goods** (6-months) at SISI Footwear Service Centre, Kanjany Road, Ayyanthole, Thrissur.
2. **Machine-shop Practice** (6 month) at Central Workshop, SISI, Kanjany Road, Ayyanthole, Thrissur.
3. **Electric & Gas Welding** (6 months) at Central Workshop, SISI, Kanjany Road, Ayyanthole, Thrissur.
4. **Fruit & Vegetable Preservation** (6 months) at SISI FP Section Kanjany Road, Ayyanthole, Thrissur.

Eligibility: Age should be between 18 to 35 years. The Candidates for training against Sl. Nos. 1 to 3 should have passed minimum 8th standard and those against Sl. No. 4 should have completed Pre-Degree course, Candidates sponsored by small scale units and having one year's practical experience in the respective trades are given preference. Entrepreneurs who have already taken steps for setting up their own units are also eligible for admission subject to the above conditions regarding age and qualifications. Selected candidates have to execute a bond for Rs. 300/-. There are 25 seats for each course.

Also offers 2-week training programme in the following Management training courses for the owners and their supervisory staff of registered small scale industries from Kerala state. Course is conducted by SISI, Thrissur in different districts in Kerala state: 1. **Industrial Management** it Tellicherry, 2. **Marketing Management** at Perinthalmanna, 3. **Quality Control** at Kozhikode, 4. **Financial Management & Cost Accounting** at Kottayam, 5. **Material Management** at Thiruvananthapuram. There are 25 seats for each course. Application forms can be can had personally or by post from Director, SISI, Kanjany Road, Ayyanthole P.O., Thrissur 680003. Only candidates from Kerala need apply. **Last date: October**.

Small Industries Service Institute, Guindy, Chennai 600032 conducts one-month Training Programme on **Market Survey for Product**

Selection and Marketing Management. Eligibility: Graduates/Diploma holders in the age group of 20-35. For more details you may contact the Deputy Director, EI/IMT, SISI, 65/1, GST Road, Channai 32.

Central Silk Board (Ministry of Textiles, Government of India) II floor, United Mansions, Mahatma Gandhi Road, Bangalore 560001 offers **Training for Non-Governmental Organisations (NGOs) in Sericulturer.**

Under National Sericulture Project, the Central Silk Board, envisages to provide assistance to selected Non-Governmental Organisations to promote the development of Sericulture. As an initial measure, the Central Silk Board offers the following courses:

1. **Short Term Training Course:** (Six months) for the field level operative of NGOs in Silkworm Rearing and Mulbery Cultivation at the Central Sericultured Research and Training Institutes, in Mysore (Karnataka) and Berhampore (West Bengal).
2. **Short Term Training Course:** (Six months) in Post-Cocoon Technology for the field level operates at the Central Silk Technological Research Institute, Bangalore.

Eligibility: Applicants should possess a Bachelor's Degree in Botany, Zoology, Agriculture (for 1), Physics, Chemistry, Mathematics/Textile Technology (for 2) and should be sponsored by the NGO. The entire training cost is borne by the Central Silk Board.

Central Institute of Fisheries Nautical & Engineering Training, P.B. No. 1724, Dewan's Road, Kochi 682016 offers various short term training courses in Fishery Technology, Fleet Management, Fishing Vessel Technology, Energy Conservation in Fishing, on board training in Outrigger Trawling and Selective shrimp fishing, Tuna long lining etc. for the benefit of Technical Officers working in Central/State Fisheries Organisations, Union Territories, Faculty members of Fisheries colleges, Technical Officers of Financing Institutions, Fleet Managers, Skippers, Engineers of Fishing Vessels owned by Public, Private Sector, etc. details of which are listed below. The Sponsoring authorities who wish to sponsor their candidates can have further details from the Director, Central Institute of Fisheries Nautical & Engineering Training, P.B. No. 1724, Dewan's Road, Kochi 682016.

Short Term Training Courses at CIFNET

1. Elementary Fishing Technology.
2. Introductory Course in Marine Fisheries Technology.

3. Fishing Fleet Management.
4. Energy Conservation in Fishing and Low Energy Fishing Methods.
5. Fishing Vessel Repairs and Preventive Maintenance Course.
6. Tuna Long Lining.
7. On Board Training in outrigger Trawling and selective shrimp fishing using underwater television and net monitoring system.
8. Refresher on Basic Navigation Chart Practice and Elementary Seamanship.

There are 10 seats in each of the above courses.

Central Institute of Plastic Engineering Technology, Chennai offers following courses:

1. Familiarisation & Operation Practice on CNC (MILL/LATHE/EDM) **Duration:** 2 Weeks. **Eligibility:** Engg. Degree/Diploma/ITI.
2. Familiarisation & Operation Practice on CMM with Computer Control. **Duration:** 2 Weeks. **Eligibility:** Engg. Degree/Diploma/ ITI.
3. Programming & Maintaining Case Studies on CNC (MILL/LATHE/ EDM) **Duration:** 2 Weeks. **Eligibility:** Engg. Degree/Diploma, ITI.
4. Identification & Selection of Plastics Materials for Product Development **Duration:** 3 Days. **Eligibility:** Unrestricted.
5. Design Tips for Injection, Compression & Transfer Moulded Plastics Components. **Duration:** 1 Weeks. **Eligibility:** Degree/ Dip. in Mech. Engg.
6. Injection Mould Design Practice using CAD (Part Time Evening) **Duration:** 12 Weeks. **Eligibility:** Degree/Diploma in Mech. Engg. 7. Processing Methods & Application of Plastics.

Further details can be had from Deputy Director CIPET, Guindy, Chennai-600032.

Indian Institute of Packaging, E-2 MIDC Area Post Box No. 9432, Andheri (East), Mumbai 400093; Plot 169 Industrial Estate, Perungudi, Chennai 600096, Block CP, Sector V, Salt Lake, Bidhan Nagar, Kolkata 700091; Plot No. 21, Functional Indl. Estate, Patparganj, Opp, Patparganj Bus Depot, Delhi 110092 offers **Two year postgraduate Diploma in Packaging**.

Eligibility: Graduate in Science (12+3) with Physics/Chemistry/ Mathematics Agriculture/Food Science/Microbiology (any two subjects) or Engineering/Technology with minimum 55% marks, Hostel facilities available. Further details can be had from above addresses. **Last date: June.**

Training Course in Testing for Diploma Holders & Science Graduates at Regional Testing Centre (NR) Min. of Industry, Govt. of India. Sahid Capt. Gaur Marg, Okhla, Near Modi Flour Mills, New Delhi-110020 (Ph: 267312671, 26312587).

Field of Testing: (i) Chemical (ii) Electrical (iii) Metallurgy (iv) Mechanical. **Duration:** 6 months. **Eligibility:** (i) B.Sc. with Chemistry for Chemical discipline (ii) Diploma in Elect./Mech./Metallurgy for the respective field of training. **Course Fee:** Rs. 4,000/- to be paid after selection. 50% concession for SC/ST/PH.

Note: Seats are limited. Admission is made on the basis of selection. No boarding and lodging facility is provided during the course.

Industrial and Technical Consultancy Organisation of Tamilnadu Ltd. 50A, Greams Road, Chennai 600006 (A joint venture of ICICI, IDBI, IFCI, SIPCOT, TIIC, SIDCO & Banks) (Ph 2829-0324/5484/4365 Fax 044-2829351̃2 E-mail itcot@vsnl.com, ramesh@itcot.com Website www.itcot.com) offers consultancy services including project reports etc. to those who wish to start their own business in various fields.

Some of the projects offered by ITCOT are as under:

1. **Project: Call Centre Overview**
   - Call Centre Operation in India/Worldwide
   - Managing for Success/Critical Success Factors
   - Information Sources about Call Centres
   - Indian/Foreign organisation connected with Call Centre establishment
   - Call Centre Technology aspects
   - 37 Case Studies
   - Project Guidelines/Financial aspects
   - 8 Seater - Local Operations Call Centre
   - 24 Seater - National Operations Call Centre
   - 50 Seater - International Operations Call Centre

2. **Project: Family Entertainment Centre**

   Leisure and Entertainment Market in India

   - Future of FECs in India
   - Facts supporting Optimism
   - Growth projection
   - FEC - Project Feasibility
   - References

3. **Projects: Fortune in Chemical Industries**

The updated report covers Introduction Properties & Uses, Process, Plant Capacity, Details of Raw Materials, Finished Goods, List of Equipments, Consumption Norms, Requirement of Utilities, Cost of Project & Means of Finance, Working Capital, Cost of Production - Profitability, Pay-Back period and Break-Even Point.

Projects Include: Aluminium Hydroxide Gel (2) Calcium Chloride (3) Dicalcium Phosphate (Feedgrade) (4) Hydroxyl Amine Sulphate (5) Phosphoric Acid (Food Grade/Technical Grade) (6) Potassium Nitrate/ Ammonium Chloride (7) Precipitated Silica (8) Ultramarine Blue (9) Tri Sodium Phosphate (10) Zinc Oxide (11) Barium Carbonate (12) Dehydrated Castor Oil (13) Guanidine Nitrate (14) Ossein (15) Sodium Hexameta Phosphate (16) Sodium Sulphate/Hydrochloric Acid (17) Potassium Silicate (New route) (18) Sodium Silicate (New route) (19) Rongalite (Sodium & Zinc Formaldehyde Sulphoxylates) (20) Zinc Sulphate/Copper Sulphate from Brassmud.

4. **Projects: Fly Ash Bricks**

   - Recycling of Paper Wastes
   - Re-refining of used Lubricant oil
   - Coconut Shell Powder
   - Vermi Composing of organic Wastes
   - Reclaimed Rubber
   - Bio Conversion of Coir pith into organic manure
   - Particle Board from Rice Husk
   - Recycling of Silk Waste
   - Pelletisation of Poultry Waste

You can get further details for several other projects from the above mentioned address.

9

Addresses of Small Industries Service Institutes & Branch SISIs etc.

Name & Address	Workshop and Lab. Facilities
ANDHRA PRADESH	
Small Industries Service Institute, Narsapur Cross Road, Bala Nagar, Hyderabad 500037.	Sand Testing Laboratory
Br. Small Industries Service Institute, F-19 to 22, Block D, IDA, Autonagar, Vishakhapatnam 530012.	General Engineering Workshop
ARUNACHAL PRADESH	
Br. Small Industries Service Institute, H Sector, P.O. R.K. Mission, Itanagar 791113.	
ANDAMAN & NICOBAR ISLANDS	
Br. Small Industries Service Institute, VIP Road, Junglee Ghat, P.O. Portblair 744103	

ASSAM

Small Industries Service Institute, Industrial Estate, P.O. Bamuni Maidan, Guwahati 781021.	Heat Treatment shops forging Machinde and Training Facilities
Br. Small Industries Service Institute Lane No. 12, Link Road, Silchar 6 (Assam).	General Engg. Workshop, Heat Treatment & Chem. Lab Testing.
Br. Small Industries Service Institute Darrant College Road, Tezpur, Sonipur (District), Assam.	Consultancy
Br. Small Industries Service Institute, Amalepatti, Diphu (Post), Karbi Anglong (District), Assam.	

BIHAR

Small Industries Service Institute, Patliputra Industrial Estate, Patna 800013.	Machine Shop, Electrical Shop, Plastic, Leather and Footwear
Br. Small Industries Service Institute, Katras Road, Matkurai, Dhanbad 826001 Bihar.	Gen. Engineering Forging and Electroplating
Small Industries Service Institute, Bela Industrial Estate P.O.R.K. Ashram, Muzaffarpur, Bihar 843116.	Gen. Engineering and Electroplating
Small Industries Service Institute, Industrial Estate, Kokar, Ranchi 834001 Bihar.	Consultancy in various trades, Technical Assistance in small scale units, Ancillary Units, Leather and Footwear Trades.

GUJARAT

Small Industries Service Institute, Harsiddh Chambers, 4th Floor, Ashram Road, Ahmedabad 380014,	Consultancy
Br. Small Industries Service Institute 1/5 Jagnath Plot, Rajkot 360001	Consultancy

HARYANA

Small Industries Service Institute, SCF-137-138, Sector 13, Urban Estate, Karnal 132001.	Consultancy
Br. Small Industries Service Institute, ITI Campus, Bhiwani 125021	General Engineering

HIMACHAL PRADESH

Small Industries Service Institute, Janak Kuti, Chambaghat, Solan 178213	Training in Glass Blowing Thermometers and Silk Screen Printing etc.

JAMMU & KASHMIR

Small Industries Service Institute, 36 B/C, Gandhi Nagar, Jammu-Tawi 180004	General Engineering & Heat Treatment
Br. Small Industries Service Institute C/o SISI Workshop, Industrial Estate, Digiana, Jammu-Tawi 180010.	General Engineering

KARNATAKA

Small Industries Service Institute, Industrial Estate, Rajaji Nagar Bangalore 560044	Tool Room, General Engineering, Heat Treatment, Glass and Ceramics, Thermometer, Chemical Laboratory

Small Industries Service Institute, Industrial Estate, Gokul Road, Hubli 580030	General Engineering Workshop
Br. Small Industries Service Institute, Mahabaleshwar, Mangalore 575003.	General Engineering Workshop
Br. Small Industries Service Institute, C-I, Industrial Estate, Gulbarga.	General Engineering Workshop

KERALA

Small Industries Service Institute, Krishna Vihar, Kanjany Road, Ayyanthole, Thrissur 680003.	General Engineering Works, Training in Footwear and Food Processing

MADHYA PRADESH

Small Industries Service Institute, 10, Industrial Estate, Pologround, Indore 452003.	Tool Room, Chemical Laboratory, Metallurgical Testing Laboratory
Br. Small Industries Service Institute, Opposite Chattisgarh Club, Civil Lines, Raipur 492001.	Technical Consultancy Chemical, Mechanical Engineering
Br. Small Industries Service Institute 7, Industrial Estate, Tansen Road, Gwalior.	Machine Shop and Heat Treatment
Br. Small Industries Service Institute M-37, Housing Board, Bodabag Colony, Rewa 486001.	General Engineering

MAHARASHTRA

Small Industries Service Institute, Kurla-Andheri Road, Saki Naka, Mumbai 400072	Tool Room, Carpentry, Chemical Laboratory, Ceramics

Br. Small Industries Service Institute, 32-33 Chikalthana, Industrial Area, Aurangabad (Maharashtra)	General Engineering
Small Industries Service Institute, CGO Complex, Seminary Hills, Nagpur 425007.	General Engineering

MANIPUR

Small Industries Service Institute, Shed No. C 17 & 18, Bit No. 23, Industrial Estate, Takyelpat, Imphal 795001.	Consultancy, Chemical Lab., Workshop

MEGHALAYA

Br. Small Industries Service Institute, Industrial Estate, Near Meter Factory, Short Round Road, Shillong 793001.	Consultancy
Br. Small Industries Service Institute, Hawakhana, Tura West-Garo Hills 794001.	Consultancy

MIZORAM

Br. Small Industries Service Institute,
Kelsih House,
Republic Veng,
Aizawal-1

NAGALAND

Br. Small Industries Service Institute, Industrial Estate Dimapur 797112.	General Engineering and Welding

ORISSA

Small Industries Service Institute, Vikas Sadan, College Square, Cuttack 753003.	Consultancy, Tool Room

Br. Small Industries Service Institute, C-9, Industrial Estate, Rourkela 769004	Machine shop, Heat Treatment
Br. Small Industries Service Institute, New Colony, Rayagada, Koraput.	General Engineering

PUNJAB

Small Industries Service Institute, Industrial Area 'B', Ludhiana 141003	Common Facility Workship, Foundry Shop, Chemical Lab., Testing, Technical Guidance and Assistance

Rajasthan

Small Industries Service Institute, 22, Godown Industrial Estate, Jaipur 302006.	Machine Shop, Mechanical Engineering Workshop

SIKKIM

Small Industries Service Institute, Tadong Housing Colony, P.O. Tadong, Gangtok, Sikkim 737102.	Consultancy

TAMIL NADU

Small Industries Service Institute, 65/1 G.S.T. Road, Guindy, Chennai 600032	Machine Shop Facilities, Metal Finishing and Testing, Technical Assistance on Various Trades
Br. Small Industries Service Institute, 151, Patel Raod, Coimbatore 641009.	Foundry and Heat Treatment, Electrical Motor Testing
Br. Small Industries Service Institute, Plot No. 76, CGE Colony, Tiruchendur Road,	General Engineering

Tuticorin 628003.

TRIPURA

Small Industries Service Institute, 21, Harish Thakur Road, Agartala 799001.	Consultancy

UTTAR PRADESH

Small Industries Service Institute, 107, Industrial Estate, Kalpi Road, Fazalganj, Kanpur 208012.	General Engineering and Heat Treatment
Small Industries Service Institute, A-208, Kamla Nagar, Agra 282005.	Technical Assistance Machine Shop
Small Industries Service Institute, E-17/18, Industrial Estate, Naini, Allahabad 211009.	General Machine Shop and Heat Treatment
Br. Small Industries Service Institute, Kham Bangla, Kaladungi Road, Haldwani 263139.	General Engineering
Br. Small Industries Service Institute, Industrial Estate, Maduadih, Varanasi 2.	General Machine Shop and Heat Treatment

WEST BENGAL

Small Industries Service Institute, 111-112, B.T. Road, Kolkata 700035.	Tool Room, Machine Shop, Heat Treatment, Ceramic Workshop
Br. Small Industries Service Institute, Station More, P.O. Suri, Birbhum 731101.	Chemical Lab.
Br. Small Industries Service Institute, Durgapur Industrial Estate, JP Avenue Durgapur 713212.	Workshop Facilities in Machine Shop, Heat Treatment

Br. Small Industries Service Institute, 3 & 4, Industrial Estate, Sevoke Road, Siliguri 734401.	Workshop in Pattern Making, Carpentry, Blacksmithy, Electroplating.

DELHI

Small Industries Service Institute, Opposite Okhla Industrial Estate, New Delhi 110020.	Tool Room, Machine Shop, Foundry, Ceramics, Electrical Testing, Lens Grinding, Heat Treatment, Electroplating, Consultancy in Chemical, Electronics, Food and Ancillary
Small Industries Service Institute, Extension Centre, Balsahyog, Connaught Circus, New Delhi.	General Engineering, Cane and Bamboo, Carpentry, Tailoring, Tinsmithy, Scooter Repairing, Electronic Servicing, Book Binding

GOA

Small Industries Service Institute, Audhi Mapari Building, (Behind Gosala Bldg.) P.O. Box No. 334 Margao 403601.	General Engineering

DADRA AND NAGAR HAVELI

Br. Small Industries Service Institute, Masat Industrial Estate, Silvassa 396230.	General Engineering

PONDICHERRY

Small Industries Service Institute, Extension Centre, Thattanchavdi, Pondicherry 605009.	General Engineering

SIB HELP LINE
PHD Chamber of Commerce and Industry
PHD House, Opp. Asian Games Village,
New Delhi 110016.
Ph: 26852416, 26863801-04 Fax: 26863135, 26568392.

117. MANUFACTURE OF TIN CONTAINERS
118. MANUFACTURE OF STORAGE TANKS, PRESSURE VESSELS, HEAT EXCHANGERS
119. MARK II HAND PUMPS
120. MARUTI WORKSHOP CUM - SERVICE STATION
121. MECHANICAL JACKS
122. METAL CUTTING DIE DESIGN
123. METAL CUTTING OF AND GRINDING WHEELS (ABBRASIVE CUTTING WHEELS)
124. METAL HOOKS & CLIPS
125. METAL SEPARATION (COPPER, TIN, LEAD) FROM SPENT WASH ACID
126. METALLIC RING JOINTS
127. METALLIC GASKET (SPIRAL WOUND)
128. MICROVEE & ABSOLUTE FILTER
129. MICROWAVE OVEN
130. MILD STEEL INGOTS
131. MINI STEEL PLANT
132. MODERN VEHICLE WORKSHOP
133. MOPED
134. M.S.HINGES
135. M.S.INGOT AND HR. STEEL STRUCTURALS
136. M.S.INGOT BY INDUCTION FURNACES
137. M.S.PIPES
138. M.S. WELDING ELECTRODE
139. MUFFLERS & SILENCERS FOR THREE WHEELERS
140. NAIL CUTTER WITH FILER & MANICURE
141. NICHROME WIRE
142. NICKEL LINED SCREENS
143. NON-FERROUS ALLOY ROLLING
144. NON-FERROUS FORGING
145. NON-FERROUS FOUNDRY
146. NON PRESSURE
147. INCANDESCENT LAMP
148. NUMBER COMBINATION LOCKS FOR LUGGAGES
149. NUTS & BOLTS
150. PAPER COATED ALUMINIUM AND COPPER WIRE
151. PETROMAX CONTAINER
152. PHOTO ETCHING OF STAINLESS STEEL PLATES
153. PIPE GALVANIZING PLANT
154. PISTON RING-AUTOMOBILE
155. PLANT PROTECTION EQUIPMENTS
156. PLATINUM LABORATORY APPARATUS
157. PRESSURE COOKER & ALUMINIUM UTENSILS
158. PRESSURE COOKER (ALUMINIUM)
159. PRESSURE DIE CASTING
160. PRINTED ALUMINIUM COLLAPSIBLE TUBES
161. PRINTED TIN CONTAINERS
162. PRINTING PRESS (CYLINDER MACHINE)
163. PUMPS FOR CHEMICAL INDUSTRY (SPECIAL)
164. RAILWAY SLEEPERS (M.S.)
165. RAZOR TWIN BLADE
166. R.C.C SPUN PIPES
167. RECONDITIONING OF M.S. DRUMS/BARRELS
168. RE-ROLLING COPPER AND BRASS SHEET AND RODS
169. RE-ROLLING MILLS
170. RESIN COATED SAND
171. RESIN CORED SOFT SOLDER WIRES
172. ROLLING MILL (BY INDUCTION FURNACE) & MANUFACTURE OF BARS, ANGLES, SQUARES, TUBES AND OTHERS
173. ROLLER BEARING & FORGING
174. ROLLING OF STAINLESS STEEL PATTA
175. RUBBER INSULATED PLIERS (HAND TOOLS)
176. RUBBING COMPOUND FOR AUTOMOBILES
177. SCIENTIFIC LABORATORY EQUIPMENTS
178. SCOOTER ASSEMBLING
179. SECONDARY LEAD EXTRAC-TION BY SCRAP BATTERY PLATES, PIPES & SHEET
180. SEAMLESS M.S. TUBES & PIPES
181. SELF TAPPING STEEL SCREW
182. SEWING NEEDLES
183. S.G. IRON & ALLOY STEEL
184. SHEET METAL PRODUCTS, (FERROUS/NON-FERROUS)
185. SHIP/MARINE CONTAINER
186. SHOCK ABSORBERS
187. SHOE EYELETS
188. SHOT AND GRITS BY AUTOMIZATION PROCESS
189. SHOVELS
190. SILICO MANGANESE ALLOYS
191. SILENCERS (MUFFLERS) EXHAUST & TAIL PIPE FOR ALL TYPES OF VEHICLES
192. SINTERED BEARING
193. SINTERED BUSHES
194. SINTERED METAL PRODUCTS
195. SOFT AND HARD FERRITES
196. SPANNERS
197. SPARK PLUGS
198. STEEL PLANT (ELECTRIC ARC FURNACE BASED- EAF)
199. SPHERIODAL GRAPHITE CAST IRON
200. SPRAY DRYER
201. STAINLESS STEEL HINGES
202. STAINLESS STEEL SHEET ROLLING TO PRODUCE STAINLESS STEEL UTENSILS
203. STAINLESS STEEL UTENSILS
204. STAPLE PINS, PAPER PIN, GEM CLIPS ETC.
205. STEEL CASTINGS
206. STEEL CHAIN
207. STEEL FOUNDRY
208. STEEL FURNITURES AND ELECTRICAL APPLIANCES
209. STEEL PLANT (MINI)
210. STEEL RODS AND COILS FROM SCRAPS
211. STEEL ROLLING MILL
212. STEEL STRIPS (COLD ROLLED) SILICON WITH GRAIN RIENTED FOR ELECTRIC USE
213. STEEL TRANSMISSION LINE TOWERS & ROLLING MILL TO PRODUCE STEEL SECTION
214. STEEL FURNITURES AND ELECTRICAL APPLIANCES
215. STEEL WIRE DRAWING AND GALVANIZING
216. STEEL WOOL
217. SUBMERGED ARC WELDED PIPES
218. SUBMERSIBLE PUMP MANUFACTURING
219. SUPER ENAMELLED COPPER WIRE
220. THREE WHEELERS
221. TIE-ROD ENDS
222. TIN CONTAINERS
223. TOOLROOM AND SHEET METAL PRODUCTS
224. TRACTOR TRAILERS
225. TRANSMISSION POWER FITTING
226. TUBULAR POLES
227. SUPER ENAMELLED COPPER WIRES
228. TUBULAR POLES FOR ELECTRICAL TRANSMISSION (BY FABRICATION PROCESS)
229. TUBULAR POLES OF M.S. & HIGH TENSILE STEEL
230. VACUUM CLEANERS
231. VACUUM FLASK (STAINLESS STEEL)
232. VALVES FOR REFRIGERA TION AND AIR-CONDITION
233. VEHICLE WELDING & PAINTING
234. VENETION BLIND
235. WASHING MACHINES (AUTOMATIC & COMPUTERISED)
236. WATER CONTROLLER (AUTOMATIC)
237. WATCH STRAPS/CHAINS/ BRACELETS/BELT BRASS & STAINLESS STEEL
238. WATER COOLERS
239. WELDED WIRE MESH
240. WELDING ELECTRODES
241. WICK STOVES
242. WIND MILL WINDOW FRAME (FERROUS & NON-FERROUS)
243. WRIST WATCH

LIST OF FEW READILY AVAILABLE 'DETAILED PROJECT REPORTS' OUT OF 30,000 REPORTS

CHEMICALS (ORGANIC & INORGANIC)

244. ACETIC ANHYDRIDE
245. ACETIC ACID FROM ETHANOL
246. ACETYLENE BLACK
247. ACETYLENE GAS
248. ACETYLENE GAS & OXYGEN (INTEGERATED UNIT)
249. ACID SLURRY BY MANUAL PROCESS
250. ACTIVATED ALUMINA
251. ACTIVATED BLEACHING EARTH (ACTIVATED FULLERS EARTH)
252. ACTIVATED CARBON FROM CASHEWNUT SHELL
253. ACTIVATED CARBON FROM RICE HUSK
254. ACTIVATED CARBON FROM RICE HUSK, COCONUT SHELL & COCONUT POWDER
255. ACTIVATED CARBON FROM WOOD
256. ACTIVATED CARBON POWDER & GRANULES FROM COCONUT SHELL
257. ACTIVATED CARBON & SODIUM SILICATE FROM PADDY & RICE HUSK
258. ALUM FOR WATER TREATMENT
259. AEROSOL INSECTICIDES SPRAY (BAYGON, HIT, MORTEIN TYPE)
260. AGARBATTI SYNTHETIC PERFUMERY COMPOUNDS
261. ALCOHOL FROM POTATO
262. ALCOHOL FROM RICE GRAINS
263. ALCOHOL FROM RICE HUSK
264. ALCOHOL FROM MOLASSES
265. ALCOHOL, BEER, STARCH, LIQUID GLUCOSE, DEXTROSE, SORBITOL, VITAMIN-C, GERM OIL, CATTLE FEED ETC. FROM MAIZE
266. ALKYD RESIN
267. ALKYLATED PHENOL LIKE NONYL PHENOL, DODECYL PHENOL
268. ALUM (NON FERRIC)
269. ALUM (FERRIC)
260. ALUMINIUM INGOT BY BAUXITE
261. ALUMINIUM PHOSPHIDE
262. ALUMINIUM PHOSPHATE
263. AMINES & ALLIED PRODUCTS
264. AMMONIA GAS
265. AMMONIA GAS BOTTLING
266. AMMONIA LIQUOR
267. AMMONIUM CHLORIDE (PURE & TECHNICAL)
268. ANILINE
269. ARGON GAS
270. ARIEL TYPE DETERGENT POWDER
271. ANTHRAQUINONE
272. ANTIMONY TRIOXIDE
273. AZODICARBONAMIDE
274. BAKING SODA FROM ASH
275. BARIUM CARBONATE
276. BARIUM COMPOUNDS
277. BARIUM PEROXIDE
278. BARIUM-THIO-SULPHATE BANZENE
279. BARYTE POWDER
280. BEER PLANT
281. BELT PASTE (WITH BFS OIL)
282. BENZYL ACETATE, BENZYL BENZOATE, BENZYL ALCOHOL
283. BETA NAPHTHOL
284. BENTONITE POWDER
285. BENZIDINE
286. BIO GAS PLANT
287. BIO GAS FILLING IN CYLINDER
288. BI-CHROMATE OF SODIUM, POTASSIUM & AMMONIUM
289. BI-FUNCTIONAL BLACK MFGR. REACTIVE DYE (DYE FROM COTTON YARN DYEING)
290. BITUMINOUS ROAD EMULSION
291. BLACK PHENYL
292. BLACK SULPHUR
293. BLEACHING POWDER (STABLE)
294. BONE CRUSHING PLANT
295. BONE MEAL (CALCINED) ENRICHMENT WITH CALCIUM & PHOSPHORUS
296. BORIC ACID
297. B.O.N. ACID
298. BRANDY
299. BUTANOL
300. 1,4, BUTANEDIOL
301. BUTYL ACETATE
302. CAFFEIN FROM TEA WASTE
303. CALCINED LIME (DEAD BURNT DOLOMITE)
304. CALCINING OF MAGNESITE & DEAD BURNT MAGNESITE
305. CALCIUM ALUMINATE
306. CALCIUM CARBIDE
307. CALCIUM CARBONATE
308. CALCIUM CARBONATE (PRECIPITATED) FROM BY PRODUCT (LIME SLURRY & CARBON DIOXIDE)
309. CALCIUM CARBONATE (ACTIVATED & PRECIPITATED)
310. CALCIUM CHLORIDE
311. CALCIUM GLUCONATE
312. CALCIUM NITRATE
313. CALCIUM SILICATE BRICKS
314. CAMPHOR POWDER (SYNTHETIC)
315. CARBON DIOXIDE
316. CARBON BLACK FROM FERTILIZER WASTE
317. CARBOXY METHYL CELLULOSE (CMC)
318. CASEIN AND BY PRODUCTS
319. CASEIN FROM MILK
320. CATIONIC SOFTNER (STEARIC ACID BASED)
321. CAUSTIC SODA
322. CAUSTIC SODA FROM TRONA
323. CAUSTIC SODA, CHLORINE AND HYDROGEN GAS BY ELECTRO-LYSIS OF BRINE SOLUTION
324. CELLULOSE ACETATE MOULDING POWDER
325. CELLULOSE POWDER & MICRO CRYSTALLINE CELLULOSE POWDER
326. CEMENT COLOUR
327. CEMENT FROM FLY ASH & LIME
328. CEMENT TILES (GLAZED)
329. DOUBLE FIRING (HEATING)
330. CHELATED ZINC (ZN EDTA)
331. CHEMICALS FROM PRAWN HEAD
332. CHITIN & CHITOSAN FROM PRAWN SHELL WASTE
333. CHLORAL HYDRATE
334. CHLORAMPHENICOL
335. CHROMIC ACID (WITH POLLUTION CONTROL)
336. CHROMIC ACID (OXIDE) & BLUE OXIDE
337. CHLORINATED PARAFFIN WAX (CPW)
338. CHROMIC ACID
339. CEMENT PAINT & DISTEMPER
340. CITRIC ACID FROM LEMON
341. CITRIC ACID FROM MOLASSES
342. CLEANING OF COOLING SYSTEM AND BOILER
343. COAL TAR DISTILLATION
344. COBALT OCTOATE
345. COMPOST FOR MUSHROOM
346. COPPER OXYCHLORIDE
347. COPPER PHTHALOCYANINE BLUE & GREEN
348. CORRECTION FLUID
349. CYANURIC CHLORIDE
350. DEFOAMING AGENT FOR PAPER INDUSTRY
351. DE-NICKELING (ELECTROLYTIC PROCESS)
352. DETERGENT CAKE & POWDER
353. DETERGENT POWDER
354. DETERGENT CONCENTRATE (IDET 10)
355. DEXTROSE MONOHYDRATE & DEXTROSE ANHYDROUS POWDER FROM TAPIOCA STARCH
356. DI-BASIC LEAD STEARATE
357. DI CALCIUM PHOSPHATE
358. DICLOFENAL SODIUM SLOW RELEASE (SR) TABLES 100MG.

359. DI ETHYL OXALATE
360. DI METHYL ORTHOPHTHALATE
361. DI-METHYL PHTHALATE
362. DICLOFENAC GEL
363. DIOCTYL PHTHALATE (DOP)
364. DI PHENYL GLYCERINE
365. DI PHENYL OXIDE
366. DINITRO-CHLORO BENZENE
367. DISTILLED WATER
368. DODECYL BENZENE SULPHONATE
369. DUSTLESS CHALK
370. EDTA & ITS SALTS
371. ELECTROLESS NICKEL PLATING ON PLASTICS
372. ENDOSULFAN
373. EPOXY RESIN BASED COMPOUND
374. ETHYL ACETATE
375. EHTYL ETHER
376. ETHYL ALCOHOL (POTABLE LIQUOR)
377. ETHYL HEXANOL
378. EXTRACTION OF ESSENTIAL OILS BY SUGAR CRITICAL FLUID (CARBON DIOXIDE) METHOD FROM FLOWERS, HERBAL & SPICES
379. FERRIC ALUM
380. FERRO CHROME LIGNO SULPHONATE
381. FERRO MANGANESE
382. FERRO SILICONE
383. FERRO VANADIUM FROM VANADIUM SLUDGE
384. FERROUS SILICATE
385. FERROUS SULPHATE
386. FERTILIZER FROM ANIMAL BLOOD & LEATHER WASTE
387. FLUORESCENT TUBE LIGHT POWDER
388. FOAMED PVC COMPOUNDING & ITS PRODUCTS
389. FORMALDEHYDE
390. FRACTIONAL DISTILLATION OF D.M.O (DEMENTHOLIZED OIL)
391. FRACTIONAL DISTILLATION OF ESSENTIAL OIL & MEDICINAL PLANT EXTRACT
392. FRICTION DUST (LIQUID & POWDER) FROM CNSL
393. FRUIT FLAVOURS
394. FURFURAL FROM RICE HUSK
395. GARLIC ACID
396. GASKET SHELLAC COMPOUND
397. GEAR OIL
398. GIBBERELLIC ACID
399. GLASS PUTTY
400. GLYCERINE
401. GOSSYPOL (POLY PHENOL) FROM COTTON SEED OIL
402. GUAR GUM POWDER
403. HAIR FIXER (HAIR GEL TYPE)
404. H - ACID
405. HENNA PASTE MAKING
406. HEPTAL DEHYDE
407. HIGH CARBON FERRO CHROME
408. HYDRATED CALCIUM SILICATE BRICK
409. HYDRATED LIME FROM SEA SHELL
410. HYDROCHLORIC ACID
411. HYDRO FLUORIC ACID
412. HYDROGEN PEROXIDE (BY AUTO-OXIDATION PROCESS)
413. ICE PACKS (SOLUTIONS TYPE, WHITE GEL TYPE, VIOLET SEMI SOLID POLYMER TYPE)
414. IMPROVING DROP POINT PARAFFIN WAX FROM 45-50ºC TO 75-80ºC
415. INDUSTRIAL ALCOHOL
416. INTEGERATED COMPLEX OF EASTER & ALLIED PRODUCTS (D.O.P, D.B.P, ETHYL ACETATE WIRE ENAMEL & CABLE JELLY)
417. IMFL (WHISKY) & COUNTRY LIQUOR
418. IRON OXIDE FOR MAKING FERITTE
419. IRON SULPHIDE
420. JUTE BATCHING OIL
421. KESH KALA TEL (HAIR DYE LOTION) (VASMOL 33, BLACK NITE TYPE)
422. L-LYSINE MONOHYDROCHLORIDE
423. LACTIC ACID FROM WHITE SUGAR BY FERMENTATION PROCESS
424. LDPE GRANULES FROM VIRGIN (LDPE RESIN)
425. LEAD EXTRACTION FROM BATTERY SCRAP
426. LEAD OXIDE (A) LEAD MONOXIDE (B) LEAD TETRA OXIDE (C) GREYLEAD OXIDE
427. LIQUID GLUCOSE & ITS BY PRODUCTS
428. LIQUID OXYGEN BOTTLING PLANT
429. LIQUID SHOE POLISH
430. LIQUID FLOOR POLISH
431. LUBE OIL VISCOSITY IMPROVED FOR P.P.G/P.E.G.
432. LUBRICANTS ASHLESS 100% COMBUSTION
433. MAGNESIUM CARBONATE AND MAGNESIUM BICARMONATE
434. MAGNESIUM HYDROXIDE POWDER
435. MAGNESIUM SILICATE
436. MAGNESIUM SULPHATE
437. MALACHITE GREEN
438. MALEIC ANHYDRIDE
439. MANGANESE SULPHATE
440. MANUFACTURING OF CARBON MONO-OXIDE WATER GAS
441. MENTHOL BOLD CRYSTALS FROM FLAKES
442. MENTHOL CRYSTAL & MENTHA OIL
443. MERCURIC OXIDE
444. METAL PRE-TREATMENT CHEMICALS
445. METHANE GAS BY SODIUM ACETATE & SODA LIME
446. METHYL ACETYL RICINOLATE
447. METOL
448. METOL FROM HYDROQUINONE & METHYLAMINE
449. MICANITE
450. MICRO NUTRIENT MIXTURE
451. MINERAL WATER
452. MINERAL WATER AND PET BOTTILNG PLANT
453. MINERAL WATER IN BOTTLES, GLASS AND POUCHES
454. MINI CEMENT PLANT (BY ROTARY KILN PROCESS)
455. MIXED FERTILIZER
456. MOSQUITO & FLIES REPELLENT AGARBATTI (INCENSE STICKS)
457. MONO CHLORO ACETIC ACID
458. MONOCROTOPHOS (TECHNICAL)
459. MOSQUITO COIL
460. MOSQUITO COIL & MAT
461. MOSQUITO MAT
462. MOTHER TINCTURE & BIO CHEMIC MEDICINES
463. NAPHTHALENE & PHENYL (INTEGRATED UNIT)
464. NATURAL MINERAL WATER BY REVERSE OSMOSIS PROCESS
465. NICKEL PLATING BRIGHTNER (PRIMARY OR CARRIER BRIGHTNER & SECONDARY BRIGHTNER)
466. NICKEL SULPHATE
467. NICOTINE FROM TOBACCO WASTE
468. NICOTINE SULPHATE FROM TOBACCO WASTE
469. NITRO BENZENE
470. NITRO CELLULOSE SANDING SEALER/LACQUER
471. NITRO MUSK
472. NITROGEN & OXYGEN GAS PLANT
473. NON-IONIC SURFACTANT (WETTING AGENT)
474. NO-CARB PASTE
475. OCTANOL
476. ORTHO NITRO PHENOL
477. OXALIC ACID FROM MOLASSES
478. OXALIC ACID FROMRICE HUSK
479. OXALIC ACID FROM TREE BARK
470. OXALIC ACID FROM WASTE VEGETABLES
471. OXYGEN GAS PLANT
472. OXYGEN GAS PLANT (AIR SEPERATION METHOD)
473. PARA-AMINO BENZOIC ACID
474. PARA-AMINO PHENOL
475. PARA TOLUENE SULPHONIC ACID
476. PECTIN FROM RAW PAPAYA
477. PERFUME (LEMON & OTHERS)

813. BREAD (AUTOMATIC PLANT)
814. BLACK PEPPER (SPICES)
815. BREAD AND BISCUITS
816. BREEDING FARM
817. BROILER CHICKEN
819. BUTTON MUSHROOM CULTIVATION & PROCESSING
820. CANNING OF RASAGULLAS IN METAL CANS
821. CAFFEIN FROM TEA WASTE
822. CANNING OF FRUITS & VEGETABLES
823. CASEIN AND BY-PRODUCTS
824. CASHEW FRUIT JUICE FROM CASHEW FRUIT APPLE
825. CASHEWNUT KERNEL EXTRACTION FROM CASHEWNUT FRUIT
826. CASHEWNUT SHELL LIQUID & KERNEL PROCESSING
827. CASHEW FENI
828. CATECHEU (BY CHEMICAL PROCESS)
829. CATTLE FEED FROM TAPIOCA
830. CHEWING & BUBBLE GUM
831. CHICKEN/SHEEP MEAT PROCESSING
832. CHOCOLATE (MILK)
833. CIGARETTE AND BEEDIES
834. COCOA BUTTER FROM COCOA MASS
835. COCONUT PRODUCTS & BY PRODUCTS PROCESS COMPLEX
836. COLD/SOFT DRINKS
837. COLLECTION OF MILK AND MILK MAKING POWDER
838. COLLECTION OF MILK AND PACKING IN POLYTHENE POUCH (1/2 KG.1 KG. & 2 KG.)
839. CONDENSED MILK (SWEETNED)
840. CONFECTIONERY INDUSTRY (TOFFEE & CANDY, SEMI-AUTOMATIC PLANT)
841. COUNTRY LIQUOR FROM MOLASSES
842. CIGARETTE
843. DAIRY FARM AND DAIRY (MILK) PRODUCTS (PASTEURISED MILK, BUTTER, GHEE, PANEER)
844. DAIRY FARM TO PRODUCE MILK & PACKING IN POUCHES (50%) & CAN(50%)
845. DAIRY FOR MILK PROCESSING
846. DAIRY FARM (BUFALO)
847. DAL (PULSE) MILL UNIT
848. DEHYDRATION OF CARROT & GARLIC
849. DEHYDRATION & CANNING OF FRUITS & VEGETABLES
850. DEHYDRATION OF FIGS
851. DEHYDRATION OF FRUITS AND VEGETABLES
852. DEHYDRATED ONIONS AND ONION POWDER
853. DRY ICE BY BREAKING OF AIR
854. DRYING OF RED CHILLIES, HALDI, DHANIA, AND GREEN PEAS
855. EGG POWDER (40,000 EGGS PROCESSING PER DAY)
856. EXPORT OF PROCESSED FOODS AND MARINE PRODUCTS
857. FISH CANNING & POUCHING
859. FISH FARMING (PRAWN & OTHER MARINE PRODUCTS)
860. FISH MEAL
861. FLOUR MILL AND MUSTARD OIL
862. FOOD COLOUR & ORASTED GROUNDNUT GRAM PEAS, ETC IN POUCHES
863. FROG LEGS PROCESSING
864. FROZEN MEATS PROCESSING
865. FOOD FLAVOURS (WHISKY) VODKA, GRAPE, BUTTER SCOTCH)
866. FOOD PRODUCTS COMPLEX (DEHYDRATED ONIONS, GARLIC POWDER & FLAKES, CATTLE FEED, TOMATO POWDER, TOMATO PRODUCTS, CANNED FRUITS & VEGETABLES, TOMATO PURE, GROUN NUT OIL, REFIND OIL, DEHYDRATED GRAPES, BANANA POWDER & WAFFERS)
867. FRUIT JUICE, JAM, JELLIES & ALLIED PRODUCTS
868. FRUIT JUICE, PICKLES PROCESSING AND CANNING
869. FRUIT JUICE MAKING & PACKING IN PLASTIC CONTAINER/POUCHES
870. FRUIT PROCESSING (JAM & JELLIES)
871. FRUIT PULP & JUICE CONCENTRATES
872. FRUIT & VEGETABLE DRYING (FREEZE DRYING METHOD)
873. GOAT & SHEEP FARMING
874. GRAM DALL/PULSE MILL
875. GRAPE DEHYDRATION
876. HARD BOILED CANDY (TOFFEE & CANDY)
877. HERBAL CIGARETTES
878. HONEY PROCESSING & PACKAGING
879. ICE CREAM OF DIFFERENT FLAVOURS
880. ICE CREAM STABILIZER
881. ICE MAKING PLANT
882. INDIAN MADE FOREIGN LIQUOR (I.M.F.L)
883. INSTANT FOOD (IDLI MIX, DOSA MIX, GULAB JAMUN MIX)
884. INSTANT FOOD (INSTANT FOOD & FAST FOOD PARLOUR)
885. INSTANT NOODLES
886. INSTANT TEA
887. INSTANT TEA FROM BLACK TEA
888. INTEGERATED STARCH BAKING POWDER/YEAST INDUSTRY
889. IODIZED SALT
890. IODIZED SALT (ORDINARY MOISTURE-LESS/FREE FLOWING IN PLASTIC BAGS AND CONTAINERS)
891. JAM, JELLIES, FRUIT JUICE & ALLIED PRODUCTS
892. KATHA AND CUTCH
893. KHANDSARI SUGAR
894. KHANDSARI SUGAR & IMFL
895. LACTIC ACID FROM WHITE SUGAR BY FERMENTATION PROCESS
896. LACTOSE & BY PRODUCTS PROCESSING FROM MILK
897. LIQUID GLUCOSE AND ITS BYE PRODUCTS
898. MACRONI AND VERMICILLI
899. MALT EXTRACTION FROM BARLEY
900. MANGO PROCESSING (MANGO PULP, JUICE & SLICES)
901. MAYUR BRAND TYPE CHEWING TOBACCO
902. MINERAL WATER
903. MILK PRESERVATION & MARKETING TO WHOLE SELLERS (INPOUCH PACKING BY UHT TECHNOLOGY)
904. MILK PROCESSING AND PACKAGING OF MILK PRODUCTS
905. MILK PRODUCTS (CASEIN, LACTOSE, GHEE & WHEY POWDER)
906. MILK TOFFEE
907. MINI FLOUR MILL
908. MINI SUGAR PLANT
909. MISRI (PEARL SUGAR CANDIES)
910. MODERN RICE MILL
911. MURABBA
912. MUSTARD OIL EXTRACTION & REFINING
913. MUTTON TALLOW
914. NAMKEEN INDUSTRY (BHUJIA, CHANA CHUR ETC.)
915. NAMKEEN & SWEETS
916. NON-BASMATI RICE FROM PADDY
917. OLEORESIN, ESSENTIAL OIL, DYES & POWDER OF SPICES
918. OLEORESIN EXTRACTION FROM DIPTERO-CARPUT TURMINATUS AND PINUS KHASYANA
919. OLEORESIN EXTRACTION FROM CHILLI
920. PAN MASALA AND POUCH

1308. DENTAL COLLEGE
1309. DENTAL GRADE EUGENOL
1310. DEXTROSE MONOHYDRATE, LIQUID GLUCOSE
1311. DEHYDRATED ONION & ONION POWDER
1312. DEXTROSE POWDER (ANHYDROUS FROM STARCH)
1314. DEXTROSE SALINE SOLUTION
1315. DISTILLERY (I.M.F.L)
1316. DISPOSABLE NEEDLES FOR SYRINGES
1317. DISPRIN
1318. DISTILLED WATER
1319. EMPTY HARD GELATINE CAPSULES
1320. FILLING & PACKING OF CAPSULES
1321. GLUCOSE - D - POWDER
1322. GLYCERINE
1323. HERBAL COSMETICS
1324. HERBAL SHAMPOO
1325. HERBAL HAIR OILS (AYURVEDIC)
1326. HOMOE & BIO-MEDICINES WITH MOTHER TINCTURE
1327. HOMOEPATHIC MEDICINES
1328. HYPODERMIC NEEDLES
1329. I.V. FLUIDS
1330. IBUPROFEN
1331. INFUSION & TRANSFUSION SETS (I.V. SET)
1332. INJECTABLE FOR PHARMACEUTICALS
1333. INJECTION AMPOULES PACKAGING BOX
1334. INTEGERATED SURGICAL COTTON
1335. ICE MAKING PLANT
1336. ICE & COLD STORAGE
1337. LACTOSE & BY PRODUCTS PROCESSING FROM MILK
1338. LICHEN (JATAMANSI CHARILA)
1339. LIQUID GLUCOSE AND ITS BY-PRODUCTS
1340. L-LYSINE MONOHYDRO CHLORIDE
1341. LIQUID GLUCOSE FROM POTATOES
1342. MEDICAL COLLEGE
1343. NICOTINE FROM TOBACCO WASTE
1344. OINTMENT-AYURVEDIC (YELLOW & WHITE)
1345. PHARMACEUTICAL AND FOOD GRADE GELATINE
1346. PHARMACEUTICAL INDUSTRY (TABLETS, CAPSULES, LIQUID, GEL, OINTMENT POWDER INJECTABLE)
1347. PHARMACEUTICAL UNIT (EOU) WITH FORMULA TIONS, INJECTABLES, ETC. PYRIDINE & DERIVATIVES
1348. SALT (IODIZED SALT)
1349. SALINE & INJECTION WATER
1350. SALINE WATER & DEXTROSE SOLUTION (I.V.FLUID IN PLASTIC BOTTLES)
1351. SORBITOL
1352. STARCH (MAIZE)
1353. SURGICAL ADHESIVE PLASTER
1354. SURGICAL BANDAGES
1355. SURGICAL GLOVES
1357. SURGICAL COTTON
1358. SURGICAL COTTON AND BANDAGE
1359. SYNTHETIC CAMPHOR POWDER
1360. TABLETS & CAPSULES
1361. TISSUE CULTURE
1362. TINCTURE FROM RECTIFIED SPIRIT
1363. TRIMETHOPIME
1364. VETERENARY MEDICINES (ONLY FORMULATIONS)
1365. VITAMIN 'C', SORBITOL' ANHYDROUS DEXTROSE, STARCH

PULP, PAPER, STRAW/GREY BOARD, KRAFT PAPER, PACKAGING, PAPER CARRY BAGE, PAPER FROM AGRO WASTE & STATIONERY ETC.

1366. AMMONIA PAPER
1367. AUTOMATIC BOOK BINDING
1368. ADHESIVE (FEVICOL TYPE)
1369. ALL PIN & GEM CLIPS
1370. CARBON PAPER
1371. CARD BOARD
1372. CARBON LESS PAPER
1373. CELLPHANE PAPER
1374. COMPUTER FORMS & SECURITY PRINTING PRESS
1375. CORRUGATED BOARD & BOX (PRINTED & LAMINATED)
1376. CORRUGATED BOARD AND BOXES FROM FROM CARD BOARDS
1377. CORRUGATED CARTONS FROM PLAIN PAPERS
1378. CORRUGATRED PACKING & MATERIAL (BULB & TUBES PACKING)
1379. DESK TOP PUBLISHING
1380. DEFOAMING AGENT FOR PAPER PLANT
1381. DRINKING STRAW PAPER
1382. D.T.P CUM OFFSET PRESS
1383. EGG TRAYS
1384. EXERCISE NOTE BOOK, REGISTER AND PAD
1385. FLEXOGRAPHIC INK
1386. GREETING CARD BY OFFSET PRESS
1387. HAND MADE PAPER FILTER PAPER
1388. HARD BOARD
1389. INJECTION AMPOULES PACKAGING BOXES
1390. INSULATIING PAPER
1391. KRAFT PAPER
1392. KRAFT PAPER FROM BAGASSE
1393. LAMINATED PACKAGING PAPER WITH PRINTING
1394. LAMINATION & COATING ON PAPER
1395. M.G. PAPER FROM WASTE PAPER
1396. MILL PAPER FROM WASTE PAPER
1397. MILL BOARD FROM RICE & WHEAT STRAWS
1398. MILL BOARD FROM WASTE PAPER
1399. MINI PAPER PLANT FROM SISAL
1400. MINI PAPER PLANT
1401. MULTI WALL PAPER SACKS
1402. NEWS PAPER FOR CHILDREN
1403. NEWS PRINT PAPER FROM RICE STRAW BAGASSE
1404. NEWS PAPER CHILDRENS
1405. NEWS PRINT PAPER
1406. OFFSET AND TREADLE TYPE PRINTING PRESS
1407. MILL BOARD BASED ON RICE STRAW
1408. PAPER AND BOARD FROM STRAW
1409. PAPER & PAPER PRODUCTS
1410. PAPER ENVELOPES
1411. PAPER CARRY BAGS
1412. PAPER BOARD CARTON
1413. PAPER CONES FOR LOUD SPEAKERS
1414. PAPER FROM AKRA
1415. PAPER FROM BAGASSE WITH CORRUGATED BOARD & BOXES
1416. PAPER FROM BAMBOO
1417. PAPER GLASSES FOR BEVERAGES
1418. PAPER FROM RICE HUSK & WHEAT HUSK
1419. PAPER FROM TREE BARK, EUCALYPRUS WOOD
1420. PAPER PRODUCTS
1421. PAPER PLANT (WHITE WRITING & NEWS PAPER FOR PULP & WASTE PAPER)
1422. PAPER PLATES, PAPER GLASS
1423. PAPER CONES & TUBES
1425. PAPER PLANT WITH DTP & PRINTING & PUBLISHING UNIT
1426. PAPER BASED PHENOLIC SHEET
1427. PAPER CUP FOR ICE CREAM
1428. PAPER TUBES SPIRAL WINDING COMPOSIT CONTAINER
1429. PAPER LABLE FOR BEER BOTTLES
1430. PARTICLE BOARD & BLACK BOARD WITH SANDING & LAMINATION OF PARTICLE BOARD
1431. PARTICLE BOARD FROM RICE HUSK
1432. POUCH FILLING & MAKING FOR TOMATO SAUCE
1433. POUCH MAKING &

Above all the Detailed Project Reports are available at *"ENGINEERS INDIA RESEARCH INSTITUTE"*. 4449, Nai Sarak (D), Main Road Delhi - 110 006
● Ph : 91-11-23918117, 2391 6431, 23840361, 31082370 ●Fax : 91-11-2391 6431
●E-Mail : eirisidi@bol.net.in

GRAVURE PRINTING

1434. PROCESSING OF PAPER FOR FEEDING IN COMPUTER

1435. PULP FROM BAMBOO & WOOD

1436. PAPER FILES

1437. PLAYING CARDS

1438. ROSIN SIZING AGENT (FOR PAPER PLANT)

1439. SAND PAPER

1440. SANITRY NAPKINS

1441. SILICON COATED PAPER

1442. STENCIL PAPER

1443. STRAW BOARD AND GREY BOARD

1444. STRAW BOARD & MILL BOARD

1445. STRAW BOARD AND PAPER BOARD

1446. TISSUE PAPER FACIAL

1447. TISSUE MOIST TOILETERY CLEANSING TISSUE AND RELATED PRODUCTS

1448. TISSUE PAPER ROLLS

1449. TETRA PACK FOR MILK PACKAGING, GHEE & OTHER LIQUIDS

1450. TOILET PAPER ROLLS

1451. TOILET PAPER & NAPKINS

1452. WAX COATED PRINTED PAPER

1453. WET FACE FRESHNER TISSUE

1454. WHITE WRITING & PRINTING PAPER

1455. WRITING & PRINTING PAPER (PAPER MILLS)

PLASTIC, B.O.P.P, ACRYLIC, DISPOSABLE PLASTIC PRODUCTS, PET PRODUCTS, P.V.C, H.D.P.E, P.P, L.D.P.E., P.U, A.B.S, THERMOFOARMING, MASTER BATCHES, & POLYMER AND RUBBER PRODUCTS, TYRE, TUBE, ADHESIVE, SHEET, COIR & MANY OTHERS

1456. ABS GRANULES FROM ABS SCRAPS FROM OLD T.V. CABINETS, WHITE GOODS ETC.

1457. ACRYLIC BEADS

1458. ACRYLIC COPOLYMER EMULSION

1459. ACRYLIC LATEX

1460. ACRYLIC SHEET

1461. ACRYLIC SHEET & MOULDED PRODUCTS

1462. ACRYLIC TEETH

1463. AUTO TUBES

1464. AUTO FLAPS FOR TRUCKS & BUSES

1465. AUTO TYRES & TUBES

1466. BABY BOTTLES (PLASTIC) WITH WHITESILICON RUBBER NIPPLES

1467. B.O.P.P. FILM

1468. B.O.P.P. PRESSURE SENSITIVE SELF ADHESIVE TAPE

1469. BABY NIPPLE (SILICON)

1470. BABY NIPPLE (BIG SIZE)

1471. BALLOON PLASTIC ADVERTISING

1472. BLISTER FILM PVC

1473. BLISTER PACKAGING & POUCH PAKAGING

1474. BLOW MOULDING PLASTIC CONTAINER

1475. COATING ON METALIZED POLYESTER FILM/METALISED PAPER/ ALIMINIUM FOIL

1476. COATING ON PLASTIC (ELECTROLYSIS) & GLASS

1477. COIR FOAM (RUBBERISED)

1478. COLOUR COATING ON PLASTICS

1479. COLOUR MASTER BATCHES FOR VARIOUS PLASTICS

1480. CYCLE TYRES AND TUBES

1481. DISPOSABLE PLASTIC CUPS GLASSES, ETC.

1482. DISPOSABLE PLASTIC SYRINGES & NEEDLES

1483. DISPOSABLE PLASTIC SYRINGES

1484. DOUGH MOULDIN COMPOUND (D.M.

1485. EPOXY RESIN

1486. EXPANDED POLYESTRENE MOULDING (THERMOCOLE)

1487. F.R.P AUTO,SCOOTER ROOFS & CEILINGS

1488. F.R.P PRODUCTS (HELMET, WASHBASIN SHEETS, ROOFING SHEETS)

1489. FIBRE REINFORCED PLASTIC (HIGH PRESSURE MOULDING WITH SMC BMC AND DMC)

1490. FIELD RUBBER CONVERTED TO THE 60% LATEX RUBBER

1491. FLEXIBLE P.U. FOAM

1492. FORMALDEHYDE CROCKERY & OTHER ITEMS

1493. FORMALDEHYDE RESIN (UREA, PHENOL,MELEMINE)

1494. GASKET SHEET

1495. GUM BOTTLE (PVC)

1496. GLASS BEADS

1497. HDPE COATED PAPER SACK

1498. H.D.P.E. BAGS

1499. H.D.P.E. CONTAINERS (BLOW MOULDING)

1500. H.D.P.E. CONTAINER, POLY JARS BY INJECTION MOULDING (FOOD GRADE)

1501. H.D.P.E. JERRY CANS

1502. HDPE MANUFACTURING FROM ETHYLALCOHOL

1503. H.D.P.E PIPE AND FITTINGS

1504. H.D.P.E. PIPES

1505. H.D.P.E PRINTED BAGS

1506. H.D.P.E TWINES AND ROPES

1507. H.D.P.E. & L.D.P.E PIPES AND FITTINGS

1508. H.D.P.E/PP BOX STRAPPING

1509. H.D.P.E/PP WOVEN SACKS USING PLAIN LOOMS

1510. HOLOGRAM STICKERS-3D

1511. H.M BAG PLANT WITH PRINTING UNIT

1512. HAWAI CHAPPALS (RUBBER)

1513. I.V PLASTIC BOTTLE

1514. ICE CREAM CUP (PLASTIC)

1515. INJECTION MOULDED AUTO COMPONENTS

1516. INJECTION & BLOW MOULDED PLASTIC PRODUCTS

1517. INJECTION MOULDED PLASTIC PRODUCTS

1518. INTEGERATED COMPLEX ESTER'S & ALLIED PRODUCTS (D.O.P,D.B.P, & ETHYL ACETATE, BUYTL ACETATE, WIRE ENAMELS, JELLY CABLE COMPOUND)

1519. L.D.P.E. (LOW DENSITY POLY ETHYLENE) GRANULES FROM VIRGIN (L.D.P.E. RESIN)

1520. INTEGERATED SURGICAL RUBBER GOODS INDUSTRY

1521. INJECTION MOULDED PLASTIC BALLS

1522. L.D.P.E FROM ETHYL ALCOHOL

1523. LDPE MOULDED PRODUCTS

1524. LAMINATION OF COEXTRUSION MULTILAYER FILM IN ROLL FORM

1525. LATEX RUBBER

1526. LATEX RUBBER CONDOM

1527. MASTER BATCHES (COLOURED, P.V.C, L.D.P.E, H.D.P.E, ETC.)

1528. MELAMINE FORMALHYDE RESIN

1529. MOULDED LUGGAGE

1530. MULTI-LAYER (3 LAYER BAGS)

1531. MULTI-LAYER (3 LAYER) FILM WITH LAMINATION & PRINTING

1532. OIL SEAL

1533. PET BOTTLE/CONTAINERS

1534. PET BOTTLES FROM PRE FORM

1535. PET BOTTLE & MINERAL WATER

1536. PET PRE-FORM FROM PET RESIN

1537. PET PRE-FORM CUM PET BOTTLES

1538. PET PRE-FORM PET BOTTLES CUM MINERAL WATERS

1539. POLY CARBONATE RESIN

1540. PTFE COMPONENTS

1541. PU/PVC SOLE FOR SPORT SHOE BY IMPORTED M/C.

1542. PVC BATTERY SEPARATOR

1543. P.V.C COMPOUNDS (FRESH)

1544. P.V.C COMPOUNDS (SCRAP)

1545. P.V.C ELECTRICAL INSULATING TAPE

1546. P.V.C. EXTRUSION PROFILES

1547. P.V.C FITTINGS

1548. P.V.C FLEXIBLE FUSIBLE POWDER HEAT FUSIBLE POWDER

1549. P.V.C GRANULES (FOR

INSULATION & SHEETS GRADES)

1550. P.V.C GRANULES FROM PVC SCRAPS (WITH POLLUTION CONTROL)
1551. P.V.C HOSES
1552. P.V.C LEATHER CLOTH
1553. P.V.C FLEXIBLE PIPES
1554. P.V.C PIPES AND FITTINGS
1555. POLYTHENE BAGS (PRINTED)
1556. PVC PLASTICS FILM SHEET SOFT/RIGID
1557. PVC RESIN AND COMPOUND
1558. PVC RULAR
1559. PVC STABLIZERS (SINGLE PACK SYSTEM)
1560. PVC WIRE AND CABLES
1561. PAPER BASED PHENOLIC SHEET FOR ELECTRICAL
1562. PHENOL FORMALDEHYDE RESIN
1563. PHENOLIC RESIN
1564. PLASTIC BEADS FROM PLASTIC SCRAPS
1565. PLASTIC BUTTONS
1566. PLASTIC CANS
1567. PLASTIC COLLAPSIBLE TUBE
1568. PLASTIC CORRUGATED SHEET & BOXES
1569. PLASTIC FILM AND SHEETS WITH PRINTING FLEXO & ROTO/LDPE/HDPE/PP/HM/PVC
1570. PLASTIC FILTER MASTER BATCH & OTHER MASTER BATCHES FOR VARIOUS PLASTICS
1571. PLASTIC JERRY CANS
1572. PLASTIC GRANULES OR POWDER FROM PLASTIC SCRAP
1573. PLASTIC INJECTION MOULDED T.V. CABINETS
1574. PLASTIC ITEMS MANUFAC TURE FROM POWDER MELAMINE
1575. PLASTIC GOODS
1576. PLASTIC PIPES & TARPAULINES
1577. PLASTIC SHEET FROM SCRAP
1578. PLASTIC PLANT (BLOW MOULDING & INJECTION MOULDING)
1579. PLASTIC PRODUCTS (GOLD, SILVER, NICKEL)
1580. PLASTIC TOYS
1581. POLYESTER BEADING
1582. POLYESTER FILM
1583. POLYTHENE BAGS & AUTOMATIC PRINTING
1584. POLYTHENE PRINTED BAGS
1585. POLYURETHANE FOAM AND ITS PRODUCTS
1586. PROPYLENE FILM (PRINTED) & BAG MANUFACTURING
1587. PLASTIC MATS
1588. RAINBOW COLOUR ON PVC FILM & SHEET
1589. RED MUD PVC PIPES AND FITTINGS
1590. RE-RUBBERISED OF SOLID TYPE
1591. RESIN COATED SAND REXINE
1592. REXINE CLOTH & ALLIED PRODUCTS
1593. RUBBER ADHESIVE
1594. RUBBER AUTO PARTS
1595. RUBBER BELTING
1596. RUBBER MOULDING UNIT INCLUDING LINING RUBBER SHEETING
1597. RUBBER RECLAIMING
1598. RUBBER ROLLERS FOR TEXTILE MILLS & PAPER INDUSTRIES
1599. RUBBER & PLASTIC SHEETS, MATS & FLAPS
1600. RUBBER SHEET AND ALLIED HOSPITAL RUBBER GOODS
1601. RUBBERIZED PVC GASKET
1602. RUBBERISED COIR
1603. RUBBER COMPOUND FOR AUTOMOBILES
1604. SAFETY BELTS
1605. SILVER AND GOLD PLATING ON PVC AND NYLON-6
1606. SILICONE RUBBER NIPPLES/ TEATS
1607. SPECTACLE FRAMES (PLASTIC)
1608. SPUNGE RUBBER
1609. SURGICAL EXAMINATION GLOVES
1610. SYNTHETIC PEARL COATING ON POLYSTYRENE BEADS
1611. SYNTHETIC RUBBER ADHESIVE
1612. TEFLON MANUFACTURING
1613. TEFLON TAPE
1614. TEFLON TAPES & CABLES
1615. THERMOCOLE SHEET AND MOULDED PRODUCTS EXPANDED POLYESTERENE EXTRUSION PROFILES
1616. THERMOFORMED PACKAGING (BLISTER PACKAGING & POUCH PACKAGING)
1617. THERMOPLASTIC POLYURETHANE
1618. THERMOFORMED CUPS, PLATES & GLASS WITH HIPS SHEET
1619. THERMOCOLE
1620. THERMOCOLE BASED DISPOSABLE GLASS, CUPS & PLATES
1621. TOOTH BRUSHES
1622. TOY BALLOON, DECORA TIVE & INDUSTRIAL BALLOONS
1623. TREAD RUBBER
1624. TYRE RETREADING (HOT)
1625. TYRE RETREADING BY COLD PROCESS
1626. TYRE TUBES & FLAPS
1627. TYRE & TUBES
1628. UNSATURATED POLYESTER FOR REXINE
1629. V-BELT AND FAN BELT
1630. VINYL ASBESTOS AND PVC WALL PAPER
1631. VITON (FLUORO ELASTOMER)

SOAP, COSMETICS & PERFUMS

1632. ACID SLURRY, SYNTHETIC DETERGENT POWDER
1632. ACID SLURRY
1633. AGARBATTI SYNTHETIC, PERFUMERY COMPOUND
1634. AFTER SHAVE LOTION
1635. ANTISEPTIC CREAM
1636. BETA IONONE
1637. BLEACHING POWDER
1638. BLUE DETERGENT POWDER
1639. CLEANING POWDER (VIMTYPE)
1640. COLD CREAM
1641. COLOURED FLAME & PERFUMED CANDLES (RED, BLUE, GREEN FLAME)
1642. COSMETIC INDUSTRY (MODERN)
1643. COSMETIC INDUSTRY (SHAMPOO, SPRAY PERFUME, TALCUM POWDER
1644. DETERGENT POWDER (ARIEL TYPE)
1645. DETERGENT POWDER (NIRMA TYPE) FULLY AUTOMATIC PLANT
1646. DETERGENT WASHING POWDER
1647. FISH OIL SOAP
1648. GLYCERINE TRANSPARENT SOAP
1649. HAIR REMOVING CREAM
1650. HERBAL COSMETICS
1651. HERBAL SHAMPO & CREAM
1652. HERBAL/AYURVEDIC COSMETICS
1653. INCENSE POWDER, INCENSE STICKS & INCENSE CAKE
1654. OPTICAL WHITENERS
1655. ROSE OIL EXTRACTION
1656. SHAMPOOS (COCONUT OIL BASED COLD PROCESS)
1657. SHAVING CREAM
1658. SINDUR (KUMKUM)
1659. SOAP COATED PAPER
1660. SPRAY DRIED DETERGENT POWDER
1661. STAIN REMOVER
1662. TALCUM POWDER (FACE & TOILET POWDER)
1663. TOILET AND HERBAL SOAP
1664. TOOTH PASTE & POWDER
1665. WASHING DETERGENT POWDER AND WASHING SOAP
1666. WASHING POWDER LIQUID DETERGENTS, LOTION & SHAMPOO

TEXTILE INDUSTRIES, READYMADE GARMENTS, COTTON, DYEING, BLEACHING, CLOTH, HOSIERY, POWER LOOM, HAND LOOM, WOOLLEN, SILK, SOCKS, SURGICAL COTTON & MANY OTHERS

1667. ANGORA RABBIT WOOL
1668. BUCKRAM
1669. CANVAS SHOES, JUNGLE BOOT, BOOT RUBBER KNEES & BOOT COMBAT
1670. CARPET FROM COTTON WASTE
1671. CERAMIC THREAD GUIDE
1672. COTTON BUDS/SWABS
1673. COTTON FROM WASTE YARN
1674. COTTON ROLLS
1675. COTTON SPIDERS FOR LOUD SPEAKERS
1676. DENIM CLOTH
1677. DENIM CLOTH (INTEGERATED UNIT WITH BLEACHING, DYEING AND PRINTING)
1678. DISPERSENT FOR TEXTILE
1679. DYEING & BLEACHING
1680. DYEING OF HANK YARN
1681. EMULSIFIER FOR WOOL BATCHING OIL
1682. EMBROIDERY ON FABRICS
1683. GARMENT DYEING, WASHING & STITCHING (JEANS, JACKETS, SKIRTS & SHIRTS)
1684. GOVES KNITTING
1685. GUNNY BAGS
1687. HDPE WOVEN SACKS
1688. HDPE TARPAULINS USING PLAIN LOOM WITH LAMINATION
1689. HDPE/PP WOVEN SACKS USING CIRCULAR LOOMS
1690. HOSIERY CLOTH (COTTON) PROCESSING (BLEACHING, DYEING, FINISHING OF CLOTH)
1691. HOSIERY INDUSTRY
1692. HOSIERY MERCERISING
1693. HOSIERY PRODUCTS LIKE VEST, BRIEF, T-SHIRTS & SOCKS
1694. JACQUARD FABRICS
1695. JUTE COIR, GRASS ROPE/ SUTLI MAKING
1696. JUTE FELT
1697. JUTE TWINES
1698. KNITTED FABRICS
1699. LAMINATED JUTE BAGS
1700. LAMINATION OF HDPE WOVEN CLOTH (JUTE,COTTON, PAPER)
1701. NYLON YARN CRIMPING, DOUBLING AND BLEACHING
1702. PIGMENT BINDER FOR TEXTILE PRINTING
1704. POLYESTER RESIN FOR WIRE ENAMEL
1705. POLYESTER RESIN
1706. POLYESTER YARN FROM WASTE POLYESTER ZIP FASTENERS
1707. POWER LOOM
1708. READYMADE GARMENTS & HOSIERY
1709. READYMADE GARMENTS MERCHANDISE
1710. READYMADE GARMENTS & COVERS
1711. READYMADE GARMENTS & EMBROIDERY OF GOWNS, SHIRTS, BLOUSES, T-SHIRTS ETC. (ONLY LADIES)
1712. READYMADE SALWAR SUIT
1713. RECOVERY OF NYLON FROM NYLON WASTE
1714. ROTARY PRINTING AND DYEING ON COTTON, SYNTHETIC TEXTILE
1715. SANITARY NAPKINS
1716. SCREEN PRINTING ON COTTON CLOTH
1717. SEWING THREAD REELS & BALLS MAKING INDUSTRIES
1718. SCREEN PRINTING ON COTTON, POLYESTER & ACRYLIC
1719. SHAWLS (WOOLLEN)
1720. SHOE LACES
1721. SILK FABRICS ON HANDLOOM
1722. SOCKS KNITTING
1723. SPINNING, DOUBLING DYEING MERCERISING & BLEACHING OF COTTON YARN
1724. SPINNING & CARDING OF WOOL INTO YARNS
1725. STARCH BOOK BINDING CLOTH
1726. SURAT JARI
1727. SURGICAL COTTON & BANDAGE
1728. SYNTHETIC TEXTILE INDUSTRY(SUITING, SHIRTING, SAREES) TERRY CLOTH
1729. T-SHIRTS
1730. TOWELS, BED SHEET COVERS
1731. TERRY TOWEL
1732. TERRY FABRICS WEAVING UNIT
1733. TEXTILE AUXILLIARIES & CHEMICALS
1734. TEXTILE BLEACHING, DYEING & FINISHING & PRINTING OF COTTON FABRICS
1735. TEXTILE (HOSIERY)
1736. TEXTILE MILL
1737. TEXTILE DYEING & PRINTING
1738. TEXTILE PRINTING (JOB WORK)
1739. TEXTILE PIGMENT PRINTING BINDER
1740. TOWEL (TERRY)
1741. VELVET CLOTH BY FLOCKING PROCESS
1742. VISCOSE STAPLE FIBRE
1743. WADDING OIL (100%) FOR WADDING OF COTTON HOSIERY CLOTH IN THE DYEING PROCESS
1744. WEAVING OF DASUTI CLOTH WITH PRINTING, DYEING, EMBROIDERY & FINISHING
1745. WASHING OF JEANS & OTHER GARMENTS
1746. WORSTED WOOLLEN YARN CLOTH
1747. ZARI GLITTER SALMA SITARA OF PLASTIC FILM

INFOTECH/IT, HOSPITALITY, HOSPITAL, COLLEGE, SCHOOL, MEDICAL, ENTERTAINMENT CLUB, WARE HOUSING & REAL ESTATE, PROJECTS

1748. AMUSEMENT PARK
1749. AMUSEMENT PARK CUM WATER PARK
1750. BANQUET HALL
1751. CALL CENTER (DOMESTIC)
1752. CALL CENTER (INTERNATIONAL)
1753. CHILDREN RECREATION CENTRE
1754. COLD STORAGE
1755. COMMUNITY HALL
1756. COMPUTER EDUCATION INSTITUTE
1757. COMPUTER SOFTWARE
1758. COLLEGE
1759. CYBER CAFE
1760. DENTAL CLINIC
1761. DENTAL COLLEGE
1762. DIAGONOSTIC CENTRE
1763. E-COMMERCE/BUSINESS
1764. E-SCHOOL (Rs. 5000/-)
1765. ENGINEERING COLLEGE
1766. ENTERTAINMENT CLUB
1767. ENTERTAINMENT CLUB, HOLIDAY RESORT, 4 STAR HOTEL, AMUSEMENT PARK CUM WATER PARK, MUSHROOM & ITS PRODUCTS, FISH FARMING, LAKE FOR BOATING, DEER PARK
1768. FASHION TECHNOLOGY INSTITUTE
1769. FAST FOOD PARLOUR
1770. FIVE STAR HOTEL
1771. FOOD PARLOUR
1772. FRANCHISE TRAINING PROGRAMME FOR IIT & ENGINEERING ENTRANCE EXAMS.
1773. GOLF COURSE
1774. HEALTH CLUB, BEAUTY PARLOUR
1775. HEALTH CLUB AND FITNESS CENTER
1776. HEALTH RESORTS
1777. HOLIDAY RESORTS
1778. HOLIDAY RESORT CUM

ENTERTAINMENT CLUB WITH 4 STAR HOTEL
1779. HOSPITALS
1780. ICE CREAM PARLOUR
1781. INTERNET SERVICE PROVIDER (I.S.P.)
1782. MEDICAL COLLEGE
1783. MEDICAL COLLEGE, HOSPITAL & RESEARCH INSTITUTE
1784. MEDICAL TRANSCRIPTION CENTRE
1785. MENTAL RETARDATION HOSPITAL & CEREBRAL PALSY
1786. MOTEL/SMALL HOTEL
1787. MULTISTOREY COMMERCIAL COMPLEX
1788. MULTISTOREY RESIDENTIAL COMPLEX
1789. NURSERY SCHOOL
1790. NATURE CARE CENTRE
1791. NURSING HOME
1792. ONLINE SHOPPING MALL (RS. 5000/- REPORT)
1793. PORTAL
1794. REHABILITATION CENTRE FOR AGED & NEEDY PERSONS
1795. RESIDENTIAL CUM COMMERCIAL COMPLEX
1796. RESTAURANT
1797. RESTAURANT WITH PUB
1798. SCHOOL (PRIMARY)
1799. SCHOOL (HIGHER SECONDARY)
1800. THREE STAR HOTEL
1801. TOURIST CLUB
1802. TRAINING INSTITUTE FOR MEDICAL TRANSCRIPTION
1803. VIDEO FILM STUDIO
1804. WARE HOUSE
1805. WEBSITE DESIGN & E-MAIL REGISTERING

AGRO BASED INDUSTRIES

1806. COAL BRIQUETTES FROM AGROWASTE
1807. FURFURALFROM RICEHULL
1808. MUSHROOM CULTIVATION & PROCESSING (BUTTON)
1809. MUSHROOM GROWING & PROCESSING WITH AIR CONDITIONING
1810. MUSHROOM CULTIVATION & PROCESSING UNIT DEHYDRATION & PACKAGING OF OYSTER & PADDY STRAW MUSHROOMS
1811. ORGANIC MANURE
1812. PAPAYA CULTIVATION
1813. PAPAYA & TOMATO CULTIVATION
1814. PROCESSING & UTILISATION OF COCONUT
1815. PROCESSING OF SHEEP HAIR TO PRODUCE WOOL

BAKERY, CONFECTIONERY & FOOD PRODUCTS

1816. AGROLACTOR SOYA MILK
1817. APPLE FRUIT JUICE WITH CANNING BOTTLING
1818. AYURVEDIC SHARBAT
1819. BAKERY UNIT (PASTRIES, BREAD, BUNS, CAKE, TOFFEE ETC.)
1820. BAKING POWDER
1821. BANANA & ITS BY PRODUCTS
1822. BANANA POWDER
1823. BANANA WAFERS
1824. BANANA CULTIVATION
1825. BEER INDUSTRY
1826. DEHULLING OF JAUN FOR BEER
1827. BEER & WINE
1828. BEER, ALCOHOL, IMFL
1829. BESEN PLANT
1830. BISCUIT PLANT
1831. BREAD & BISCUIT PLANT
1832. BOTTLING PLANT COUNTRY LIQUOR FROM RECTIFIED SPIRIT
1833. BRANDY
1834. BREAD RUSKS
1835. CANNED FRUITS & VEGETABLES
1836. CANNING & PRESERVATION OF MEAT
1837. CANNING & PRESERVATION OF VEGETABLES
1838. CANNING OF MANGO PULP & MANGO SLICES
1839. CARBONATED BEVERAGS
1840. CASHEW FENI
1841. CASHEW NUT (DRIED & FRIED)
1842. CATTLE BREEDING
1843. CATTLE BREEDING & DAIRY FARM TO PRODUCE MILK
1844. CATTLE FEED FROM TAPIOCA
1845. CHEWING GINGER & AMLOKI
1846. CHEWING GUM
1847. CHILLI SAUCE
1848. CHILLI POWDER
1849. CHOCOLATE
1850. CIDER PLANT
1851. COCOA POWDER
1852. COCOA BUTTER & COCOA POWDER
1853. COCONUT SHELL POWDER
1854. COCONUT WATER
1855. COCONUT SWEET (WATERY)
1856. COCONUT MILK POWDER (DEHYDRATED)
1857. COCONUT PRODUCTS & BY PRODUCTS (INTEGRATED PLANT)
1858. COLD DRINK
1859. CURRY POWDER
1860. DAIRY FOR MILK PROCESSING (GHEE, BUTTER & PANEER)
1861. DAIRY PRODUCTS
1862. DAIRY PRODUCTS MILK PACKAGING IN POUCH (GHEE, BUTTER, ETC.
1863. DAIRY FARM TO PRDUCE MILK WITH PACKAGING (COW)
1864. DAIRY FARM TO PRDUCE MILK WITH PACKAGING (BUFALLOE)
1865. DAIRY FARM & MILK PRODUCTS
1866. DAL MOTH, CHANACHUR & BHUJIYA
1867. DEHYDRATION OF FRUITS & VEGETABLE
1868. DESICCATED COCONUT POWDER FROM COCONUTS
1869. DEHYDRATION & CANNINGOF FRUITS & VEGETABLES
1870. DRY FRUIT ROASTING & PACKAGING
1871. DRYING OF RED CHILLIES, HALDI, DHANIYA, PEAS & GROUND NUT
1872. EGG POWDER
1873. FISH CANNING IN TIN & POUCHES
1874. FISH DEHYRATION (DRYING OF FISH)
1875. FISH MEAL
1876. FISH PROCESSING (BEAST FREEZING PROCESSES)
1877. FLAVOURS FOR FOOD INDUSTRIES
1878. FLOUR MILL (ROLLER)
1879. FROZEN MEAT
1880. FOOD DEHYDRATION (FRUITS & VEGETABLES)
1881. FRIED & ROASTED GROUND NUT, GRAMS, PEAR ETC.
1882. FRUIT JUICE MAKING & PACKAGING IN PLASTIC CONTAINER
1883. FRUIT JUICE IN TETRA PACK (DRINKS)
1884. FRUIT JUICE, SQUASHES, SAUCE & KETCHUP, JAM, JELLY, VINEGAR ETC.
1885. GARLIC FLAKES
1886. GARLIC POWDER
1887. GHEE & BUTTER
1888. GINGER (PULVERISED)
1889. GINGER GLAZING & PRESERVATION
1890. GINGER STORAGE
1891. GINGER PROCESSING
1892. GINGER OIL & GINGER DUST
1893. GINGER POWDER (DRY) & OLEORESIN
1894. GRAPE DEHYDRATION
1895. GRAPE CULTIVATION
1896. GRAPE JUICE
1897. HONEY PROCESSING & PACKAGING
1898. ICE CREAM & ICE CANDY
1899. ICE CUBE
1900. INVERT SUGAR
1901. IDLI MIX, DOSA MIX SAMBHAR MIX, VADA MIX, GULAB JAMUN MIX
1902. INSTANT COFFEE & INSTANT TEA

Above all the Detailed Project Reports are available at *"ENGINEERS INDIA RESEARCH INSTITUTE"*. 4449, Nai Sarak (D), Main Road Delhi - 110 006

• Ph : 91-11- 23918117, 2391 6431, 23840361, 31082370 •Fax : 91-11- 2391 6431

•E-Mail : eirisidi@bol.net.in

1903. INSTANT NOODLES
1904. INSTANT SOUPS
1905. IODIZED SALT FROM CRUDE SALT
1906. JAM CHUTNEY PICKLES & SQUASHES
1907. KATHA MANUFACTURING
1908. LECITHIN (SOYA BASED)
1909. LEMON & ITS PRODUCTS
1910. MACARONI MANUFACTURING
1911. MACARONI, SPAGHETTI, VERMICELLI & NOODLES
1912. MAIZE & ITS BY PRODUCTS MALTING PLANT
1913. MANGO PAPPAD (AAM PAPPAD)
1914. MANGO POWDER RIPE
1915. MANGO POWDER
1916. MANGO PROCESSING & CANNING (MANGO PULP)
1917. MEAT PROCESSING (CHICKEN MUTTON)
1918. MEAT PROCESSING (BUFFALO)
1919. MENTHOL BOLD FROM MENTHOL FLAKES
1020. MILK POWDER
1921. MILK POWDER & GHEE
1922. MILK POWDER, GHEE & SPICES
1923. MILK PRESERVATION & MARKETING TO WHOLE SELLERS
1924. MILK PRESERVATION & MARKETING TO WHOLE SELLERS (IN POUCHES)
1925. MILK TOFFEE MANUFACTURES
1926. MINERAL WATER
1927. MINERAL WATER IN POUCHES
1928. MINI FLOUR MILL ATTA MAIDA, SUJI & WHEAT BRAN
1929. MITHAI/HALWAI (SWEET & NAMKEEN)
1930. MUTTON PROCESSING
1931. PAN MASALA (MEETHA, SADA, ZARDA) MAKING & PACKING
1932. PAN MASALA AND POUCH MAKING
1933. PANEER (CHEESE)
1934. PAPAD & BARIYAN
1935. PAPAD PLANT
1936. PEPSICOLA IN POLYTUBES
1937. PETHA PACKAGING
1938. PICKLES
1939. PIGGERY/MEAT/CHICKEN PROCESSING
1940. PINE APPLE JUICE CANNING
1941. POTATO & ONION POWDER
1942. POTATO & ONION FLAKES
1943. POTATO CHIPS
1944. POTATO GRANULES
1945. POUCH FILLING FOR SAUNF SUPARI ILAICHI ETC.
1946. PRESERVATION OF RAWS MANGO JUICE
1947. PROCESSED CHEESE & MARINE PDTS.
1948. PULP FROM TARMARIND
1949. READYMATE PROCESSED FOOD
1950. RICE & CORN FLAKES
1951. RICE BASMATI (TRADING)
1952. RICE POLISHING & PACKAGING IN POUCH
1953. ROASTED/SALTED/MASALA/ CASHEW NUTS ALMONDS & PEA NUT
1954. ROLLER FLOUR MILL

INFOTECH/IT PROJECTS

1955. MEDICAL TRANSCRIPTION
1956. E-COMMERCE
1957. CYBERCAFE
1958. INTERNET SERVICE PROVIDER (ISP)
1959. COMPUTER EDUCATION CENTRE
1960. PORTAL (WEBSITE DESIGN)
1961. CALL CENTRE

TERMS AND CONDITIONS

FOR INDIA

1. Please ask for Quotations of Each *Market Survey Cum Detailed Techno Economic Feasibility Report.* Payable in advance through Draft/M.O./Cash in favour of 'ENGINEERS INDIA RESEARCH INSTITUTE', Delhi. Delivery by Regd.post within 2 Days. (Postage Free)

2. Ask for the Hi-Tech Projects Monthly magazine. Each Magazine covers many Project Profiles for selection of Industry.

FOR OVERSEAS

1. Please ask for Quotations in US $ of Each *Market Survey Cum Detailed Techno Economic Feasibility Report.* Payable in advance through Draft/M.O./Cash in favour of 'ENGINEERS INDIA RESEARCH INSTITUTE', Delhi. (Payable in India) Delivery by Regd.post within 4 Days.

2. Ask for "Hi-Tech Projects" Monthly magazine. Each Magazine covers many Project Profiles for selection of Industry.

ENGINEERS INDIA RESEARCH INSTITUTE

Add: 4449, Nai Sarak (D), Main Road, Delhi - 110 006 (India)
Ph:. 91-11-23918117, 23916431, 23840361, 98114-37895
Fax: 91-11-23916431 E-Mail : eirisidi@bol.net.in
Website:www.eiriinia.org
Also at : 4/27, Roop Nagar, Near Roop Nagar No. 1 School, Delhi - 110 007 (India) Ph:. 23840361